Guide to the LECTIONARY

John H. Fitzsimmons

MAYHEW-McCRIMMON
Great Wakering Essex England

First published in Great Britain in 1981 by
Mayhew-McCrimmon Ltd
Great Wakering Essex England

First edition 1981

ISBN 0 85597 314 5

Edited by Hugh J. McGinlay & Robert B. Kelly
Lithographic artwork by Graphitti
Cover design by Paul Shuttleworth
Printed by Mayhew-McCrimmon Printers Ltd

Contents

Quotations from official texts are indicated by the initials of the documents' Latin title:

CR = ***Calendarium Romanum***
The Roman Calendar,
revised in the light of Vatican II,
promulgated 1969.

DV = ***Dei Verbum***
The Dogmatic Constitution on Divine Revelation,
of Vatican II,
promulgated 1965.

IGMR = ***Institutio Generalis Missalis Romani***
The *General Instruction* which prefaces
the *Roman Missal* of Paul VI,
promulgated 1969.

LMOG = ***De Lectionarii Missae Ordinatione Generali***
The *praenotanda* which prefaces
the *Lectionary,*
promulgated 1969.
All references are to the first (1969) edition.

MPC = ***Mysterii Paschalis Celebrationem***
The *motu proprio* of Paul VI (14 Feb 1969)
promulgating the *Calendarium Romanum.*

SC = ***Sacrosanctum Concilium***
The Constitution on the Sacred Liturgy
of Vatican II,
promulgated 1963.

What is the Lectionary?

What is the Lectionary?

One of the more dramatic aspects of the current renewal of the Church has been the flowering of interest in the bible. Study groups, adult education courses, bible services, and a whole host of other facets of contemporary Church life make it clear that the scriptures have been given a prominence in Catholic worship, devotion, and practice which they did not always have.

The most obvious sign of this has been the emphasis placed on the Word of God in the church's liturgy. The Mass itself, the sacraments, and all other forms of liturgical worship have been revised, and a notable feature of the revision has been the introduction of the 'liturgy of the word'.

For some people this is a cause for genuine consolation; for many others, however, it is a cause for consternation, because they feel themselves ill-equipped to grasp the meaning of so much that is unfamiliar to them.

The first and clearest evidence of the important place held by the Scriptures in the liturgy is the Lectionary, i.e. the full and official collection of biblical readings for liturgical celebration in the Church. Originally published in 1969, it stands as one of the decisive contributions to the Vatican II programme of reform, and yet perhaps it is one of the least understood.

The origins of the lectionary are to be sought in the insistent request of the bishops at Vatican II that **'a more representative portion of the scriptures be read to the people over a set cycle of years'**; the council also hoped that the word of God would be opened up **'more lavishly, so that richer fare may be provided for the faithful'**. In presenting the Lectionary and the missal to the Church as a response to these wishes of the Council, Pope Paul VI remarked that the whole purpose was that 'sacred scripture will be a perpetual source of spiritual life, the chief instrument for handing on Christian doctrine, and the centre of all theological study'.

For the intentions of the Pope and the Council to become reality, the whole community must recognise and understand what the Lectionary is trying to do and understand the principles on which it is built.

THE PRINCIPLES OF THE LECTIONARY

Three-year cycle

The first principle of the Lectionary is that the Word of God is proclaimed in the Church over a ***cycle of three years***: it is very important to grasp that it is one unified cycle, not three set side by side — therefore, the impact and content of the readings are to be judged by their 'cumulative effect' over the whole period.

The intention which the composers of the Lectionary had was to fulfill the wishes of Vatican II: **'to make sure that the more important parts of the bible would be proclaimed on Sundays and solemnities, days when the Christian people are bound to celebrate the Eucharist together. In this way, the faithful will be able to hear the main themes of the revealed Word of God over a period of time'** *(SC35; LMOG1)*.

Gospels central

The second principle of the Lectionary is ***the centrality of the gospels***. This is quite logical, because Vatican II reaffirmed the faith of the Church that the gospels remain **'our principal source for the life and teaching of the incarnate Word, our Saviour'** *(DV18)*. What this means in practice is that each year of the cycle is characterised by one of the three synoptic gospels;

the first year of the cycle is built around the Gospel of Matthew;

the second year of the cycle concentrates on the Gospel of Mark;

the third year revolves around the Gospel of Luke.

Put another way, this means that instead of being left with A — B — C, we are in reality confronted with ***the Year of Matthew, the Year of Mark,*** and ***the Year of Luke.*** For the period covered by the Ordinary Sundays of those years, it is the individual Gospel which sets the pattern and controls the themes of the liturgy. This means in practice that for 33 or 34 Sundays out of the 52, our preaching and instruction has to be guided by the evangelists.

The beauty of this is that it allows each of the Gospels to speak for itself; it means that the particular theological interests of each of the evangelists have a chance to express themselves; it means that the inspiration for preaching can be derived from the different Gospel portraits of Christ in turn. There is the further point to be made in this connection that it reflects what present-day biblical scholarship is doing. We live in an age which has moved beyond the comparative study of the Gospels in order to concentrate on the personal and individual theologies of each evangelist. There is no need for us to be bogged down in the technicalities of the matter; it is clear enough that there are enormous pastoral possibilities in this approach. All that is required is that we develop an appreciation of what those theologies are.

If we look at each of the three years of the cycle in relation to the Gospel which stands at their centres, then it will be clear *how* taking the principles of the Lectionary to their logical conclusions can provide us with the key to understanding the whole thing. In trying to discern the contribution of each of the evangelists to the Gospel Tradition, we are putting our finger on what they have each to give to the Church's liturgy and to our preaching.

YEAR OF MATTHEW (YEAR A)

In the case of Matthew's Gospel, there is no immediate problem; he shows an interest in the *words* of Jesus which is unmatched by the others. It is for this reason that many people found Pasolini's film on

Matthew's Gospel so 'wordy', but at least the director was being faithful to his script. Matthew's portrait of Christ is essentially that of the Master, the Teacher of the New Law. This explains why from an early age, almost by instinct, the Church turned to Matthew for the teaching of Christ. What the evangelist has done is to gather together the traditions of the words of Christ and to enshrine them in five major discourses or 'sermons'. It is these five sermons which constitute the skeleton of the Gospel:
the Sermon on the Mount (*Chapters 5-7*),
the Mission Sermon (*Chapter 10*),
the Parable Sermon (*Chapter 13*),
the Community Sermon (*Chapter 18*),
the Final Sermon (*Chapters 23-25*).

It is principally in these sections that we are to discover Matthew's message, for they stand at the heart of the work and everything else is built around them.

It comes as no surprise to find that these are the best represented parts of the Gospel of Matthew in the Lectionary for Year A. If we are going to take them, and the intention of the Lectionary itself, seriously, then they should be the primary source for preaching and catechesis in the course of the first year of the liturgical cycle. The narrative sections which are placed in between the five sermons have been composed by the evangelist in such a way that there is a coherence in the whole work: discourse and narrative stand side by side, so that the narrative chapters prepare the way for what comes in the discourses.

Underlying the whole of the first Gospel is the evangelist's conviction that the Lord is *with* his Christ 'always — to the end of time'. It is the sense of the abiding presence of Christ, whom he defines as *Emmanuel* (God-with-us), that has guided Matthew most in his work. This explains again why for centuries this has been known as the 'ecclesial Gospel'. The nature of the Church, or what Vatican II called the 'mystery of the Church', and the abiding sacramental presence of Christ — these are the two poles of the theology of Matthew. It is there, we ought to concentrate attention; it is from there that we have to derive our instruction from week to week in the course of Year A. The universal catechesis of the Church during that year is inspired by Matthew, and his interests and concerns are intended to become those of the Church. We can hardly do less than make them ours as well. In developing the Lectionary's presentation of Matthew's insight into

Christ and his message, we have an opportunity to consider with our communities the reality of 'Christ the sacrament of encounter with God'. In short, we might say that through this Gospel we are invited to deepen our understanding of *ecclesiology* and *sacramental theology.*

THE YEAR OF MARK (YEAR B)

When we turn to the Gospel of Mark, we are faced with a very different work. There is not the same organised, almost artificial presentation of the story of Jesus that we have in Matthew. The atmosphere of Mark is more direct, more personal, more 'primitive'. In the past, this has led many people to think that this Gospel is somehow untheological; however, in recent times, it has become clear that Mark's simplicity is only superficial. This Gospel enshrines a theology which is at once challenging and profound, because it seeks the answer to one single question — 'Who do you say that I am?' Time and time again, Mark brings us face to face with the mystery of Christ himself, Son of God yet Son of Man.

It is probably true to say that we know more about Mark than we do about any of the other Gospel writers. The crucial point in his career is his association with Peter; he is described as Peter's catechist or interpreter; Peter must then feature as an important source for his version of the story of Jesus. This may well explain why there is in his Gospel so much material that can only be classified as 'Eye witness account' or 'Narrative based on personal testimony'.

There is a certain wryness on the part of many of the Fathers of the Church in commenting on the Gospel of Mark — to them it seemed formless and 'without order'; no doubt many of us will feel the same about it. Indeed, there are as many 'plans' of the Gospel as there are writers, and some have even despaired of being able to provide an intelligible outline. However, the main lines of Mark are not too hard to discern.

He begins by introducing his main interest — the person of Jesus himself; he follows Jesus through his ministry in Galilee, outside of Galilee, and in Jerusalem; he dwells at some length on the passion and resurrection. Simple enough, at least in basic shape. The crisis or turning-point is easily recognised: it is the confession of Peter and the first prediction of the passion (*8:27-33*). From that point onwards the teaching of Jesus is that the Son of Man 'must suffer', and this teaching is directed almost exclusively to the disciples themselves. This is why Mark has been described as 'a passion story with an introduction'.

All through, the evangelist's intention is to bring his readers face to face with Christ, and in so doing he is not afraid to present us with the humanity of Christ in all its starkness. All that Mark says is geared to the answering of the question 'Who is this?' or 'Who do you say that I am?' To communicate the full mystery, he uses the two titles 'Son of God' and 'Son of Man'; these, then, are the two poles of his theology. In short, we might say that in following the Gospel of Mark through Year B, the Lectionary is giving us the chance to deepen our *christology*. The personal quality of Mark's portrait of Jesus must translate itself into the personal quality of our faith — that is what the Church asks of us in that part of the cycle.

YEAR OF LUKE (YEAR C)

The Gospel of Luke is everybody's favourite. It has been remarked just how often Franco Zeffirelli turned to it for inspiration in his film, *Jesus of Nazareth*. Maybe this stems from the fact that it was written for people like us whose roots are not in Judaism. It reflects the teaching of a Church that was striving to open up the Gospel message to the world of paganism. That certainly explains why Luke places so much emphasis on the universal appeal of Jesus; it explains why there is a long line of writers who have found the Christ of Luke so attractive, from the earliest times. Dante described Luke as the 'scribe of the gentleness of Christ', and in our own time W. D. Davies has written: 'The Jesus of Luke, one feels, might well have uttered the words written on the Statue of Liberty in New York harbour — "Give me your tired, your poor, your huddled masses yearning to breathe free. Send these, the homeless, tempest-tost to me".' But, as in everything that Luke wrote, there is a parallelism at work in his portrait of the Saviour. Indeed, his portrait is more in the nature of a diptych, and both sides have to be taken together for completeness. The picture of the merciful, compassionate Christ is balanced with an insight into one whose mission is urgent and whose time is short. This expresses itself in the total demand that Jesus makes of those who would follow him, and explains why Luke's is the Gospel of renunciation and perseverence. What Luke offers us then is a catechism of christian discipleship — with its joys and consolations and its difficulties and temptations. Both sides belong equally to the picture — they do not cancel out one another, but are complementary.

Saint Luke's own character comes out quite well when we consider his work, remembering that what he wrote was, in fact, a two-volume account: the *Gospel* and the *Acts of the Apostles*. A crucial factor is his insight in his association with Saint Paul (just as the association with Saint Peter was crucial in the case of Mark); it may well be the influence of Paul's vision of Christ's reconciling work which has coloured his Gospel to the point where it is clearly the Good News for the poor, the outcast, and the underprivileged. Luke tells us that he set out to write 'an ordered account', 'after carefully going over the whole story from the beginning' (*1:3*). The idea that enabled him to get everything into order and perspective was the idea of *movement* or *direction*. So, his work moves from Galilee to Jerusalem (*Gospel*) and from there 'throughout Judaea and Samaria, to the ends of the earth' (*Acts — cf. 1:8*). In this framework he has told his story in such a way that it could well be resumed in this one sentence: 'Jesus Christ is the Saviour of men'.

After the Infancy Gospel (*chapters 1-2*) he tells the story of the Galilean Ministry (*chapters 3-9*) in a way which is roughly the same as Matthew's and Mark's, though even here he has his own interests, his own theological insight. It is only when he comes to the end of the Galilean Ministry that he really shows his hand: from that point onwards, Jesus, and the Gospel, are 'on the move'. The whole of the Central Section (*chapters 9-19*) is cast in the mould of a 'Travel narrative', describing the journey of Jesus to Jerusalem, to death and resurrection. What is significant about this central part is the fact that in it Luke has gathered together everything that he has to contribute to the Gospel Tradition. Here we will find all the parables, stories, controversies and miracles that he tells us of and nobody else does. The rest of the Gospel (*chapters 20-24*) rejoins the common tradition, even though Luke continues to tell the story in his own way.

Clearly, then, the emphasis of his theology is to be found in the 'Travel Narrative'; significantly, 19 of the 33 passages in the Lectionary for Year C come for this section. Luke's vision of the journey of Jesus is not a geographical or chronological affair; he is not particularly interested in the details of time and place. What he is interested in is that the journey should be seen as an itinerary for the Church and for the individual Christian. 'The journey to Jerusalem is the way to suffering and glorification. But Jesus is not alone. His disciples accompany him on the journey and are bound through him into a community . . . The way Jesus walks is unique, but his disciples may follow after him along it.' Taking all of these factors into account, it seems that we might consider the Gospel of Luke as the opportunity to preach about *the Christian Life.* The evangelist goes out of his way to show us what it means to be a follower of Jesus. To spell that out, and to follow up its implications is really the task of the preacher in the course of Year C. The rich, the poor, the lonely, the busy, the housewife, the business man, the judge . . . they will all find in Luke's Gospel the indications they need to reduce the word of Christ to their own situation.

Seasons

The third underlying principle of the Lectionary is its ***clear distinction between the major seasons of Lent-Eastertide and Advent-Christmas, and the rest of the year, known as 'ordinary time'.***

During the major seasons there is a clear concentration on the specific mysteries of the Church's faith:
the passion-resurrection during Lent-Easter;
the incarnation during Advent-Christmas.
This means that the biblical readings all refer to that mystery, and they do so in a way that is definitely *thematic.* They are all tied together, and they go together to highlight one or other aspect of the mystery that is being celebrated. There is, therefore, a real sense of coherence about the readings at these times; in a sense, they are easy to handle because they are all of a piece, and because they all come from traditional sources:
from John for Lent-Easter
from Isaiah, Luke 1 & 2 and Matthew 1 & 2 for Advent-Christmas.

LENT-EASTER
THE SEASON OF JOHN

It is only when we turn to the 'thematic' principle of the Lectionary, which comes into its own in the major seasons of the liturgical year, that we discover the importance of the Gospel of John. This is very clear in connection with Lent and Easter. As the introduction to the

Lectionary says: **'the tradition of both east and west has been preserved by which the Gospel of John is read in the final weeks of Lent and throughout Easter time, because it is the "spiritual" Gospel in which the mystery of Christ is sounded out to greater depths.'**

The season of Lent is celebrated with two principal and inter-related ideas in mind. In the words of Vatican II: **'the Lenten season has a twofold character:**

1. it recalls baptism or prepares for it;

2. it stresses a penitential spirit.' *(SC 109).*

The latter was familiar enough — but the baptismal aspect less so. The liturgy has been renewed in such a way that the *baptismal* will be perceived more clearly. Vatican II mentioned it as part of the programme of revision and so it is that **'those important passages from the gospels which were read to catechumens in the early centuries to prepare them for baptism are proclaimed. These readings are directed to *all* the faithful, because during Lent the whole Church, along with those about to be baptised calls to mind the mystery of its initiation into Christ.'** The baptismal character of *Easter* is clearer to us, and we are constantly reminded of the connection between baptism and the Paschal Mystery in the new rite. Throughout the centuries, the Gospel of John has been the inspiration of the Church's lenten and paschal catechesis; the greater our understanding of this evangelist and his work, the greater will be the benefits we will derive from the yearly celebration of the central mysteries of our faith.

There are many people who shy clear of the fourth gospel because they think it is too deep and too difficult; there are those, too, who think that the evangelist writes not at all clearly, and that he repeats himself with a stately measured style that does not suit their taste. To some extent, of course, this is true. Yet, the more familiar we become with John's Gospel, the more these difficulties recede into the background. One recent commentary has put it well: 'The eloquence, nobility, and persuasiveness of John's story have not lessened down the years, for it is still the Gospel of John that speaks most tellingly to the simple believer, and also most effectively plumbs the depths of Christian belief and commitment for the highly sophisticated. For all men, it still bears the powerful witness that "Jesus is the Christ, the Son of God", and enables men 'believing, to have life in his name".' (J. Marsh, *Pelican Commentary on St John,* 1968)

A handy summary or synthesis of the Gospel of John will be found in the idea of 'life'. The fullness of life, which is characteristic of God himself, is incarnate in Christ and through the humanity of the Word is communicated to men. This basic idea explains why the personal encounters of John feature so much in the liturgy of Lent and Easter; each of them illustrates in some way the fullness of life, explains how baptism is the sacrament of life, the beginning of 'grace'. The connection between baptism and the resurrection is worked out too: every incident in the Gospel is charged with the power of the risen Lord, and the life that he gives is already an 'eternal life'. Therefore, in the Gospel of John, we can discern a theology of grace which is worked out, not in abstract ideas, but rather through the experience of individuals like ourselves. This must remain the key instrument to a fuller understanding of the paschal mystery.

ADVENT-CHRISTMAS

The 'thematic principle' is also at work in the Lectionary's presentation of the word of God during *Advent and Christmas*. This means that the whole season is a unit, with a clear purpose and an equally clear unfolding of its major themes. It means, further, that each of the sets of three readings has a single theme, unlike the Ordinary Sundays where the middle reading sticks out like the proverbial sore thumb. If we concentrate on the Sundays of Advent, we discover the following pattern:

—the second coming in glory of the Lord at the end of time (First Sunday);
—the preaching of John the Baptist (Second & Third Sundays);
—the events immediately preceding the birth of our Lord (Fourth Sunday);

As a backdrop to all this, there is a constant refrain from the Old Testament — the whole range of messianic prophecy, drawn mainly from Isaiah. During Christmas the mystery of the incarnation itself is presented from all sources: the four Gospels, the theology of Saint Paul, the Letter to the Hebrews, the First Letter of John. The trouble with this period of the year is that it is extremely busy; we are taken up with so many different interests that the liturgical season can be submerged in a sea of other peripheral celebrations. Liturgically, this time of the year is every bit as hectic, and we have to be careful lest it go by default. The preparation required, therefore, is at least a gentlemen's acquaintance with the Book of Isaiah and the Infancy

Gospels of Matthew and Luke. Everything else is built upon that foundation. With that kind of preparation, there is no danger of the central mystery of the incarnation's disappearing under the surface.

Systematic catechesis

In an age when many lament the passing of the catechism, it is strange that they do not realise that the Church still has its own programme of catechetical instruction, set into the framework of the liturgy. It is very sad that few, whether at primary, secondary or tertiary level have turned to the Church's presentation of the Word of God for inspiration in devising 'new' styles of religious instruction.

Yet, the preface to the Roman Missal of 1969 is quite clear on the point: the Lectionary was composed so that the desires of the bishops at Vatican II could be fulfilled and that **'sacred scripture will then be a perpetual source of spiritual life, the chief instrument for handing down Christian doctrine, and the centre of all theological study.'** If we take this seriously, there are almost unlimited possibilities for relating theology and catechetics to the liturgy of the Church's year. The following is one way of representing these possibilities:

Year of Matthew (Year A):
- The incarnation (Advent-Christmas)
- The Church and the sacraments (Matthew)
- The life of grace (John)

Year of Mark (Year B):
- The incarnation (Advent-Christmas)
- The mystery of Christ and faith (Mark)
- The life of grace (John)

Year of Luke (Year C):
- The incarnation (Advent-Christmas)
- The Christian life; the social gospel (Luke)
- The life of grace (John)

Expressed this way, it is clear that what we have in the liturgy over the three-year cycle is a comprehensive presentation of Christian doctrine. This is a consolation and a challenge: a consolation because it destroys any fears that we might be missing out on something (for there is not an element in theology or doctrine which is not reducible to these areas); it is a challenge, because the educative process means that these basic, evangelical, ideas have to be expanded and applied to the lives of our communities in the light of 2,000 years experience and development.

This is not to say that the Lectionary is merely a programme of christian instruction: rather, the growing understanding of faith experienced within the community of christian believers is directed through the Lectionary by the Gospel itself. The Gospel itself, then, becomes the pattern, or 'system' for the catechesis of the community.

This is no mean task. In the long run, it demands that every priest, deacon, and teacher will have to give an account of the faith that is theirs in the light of the gospel, and that is a challenge indeed. But, until that is done, there is no real hope of the word of God's being opened up **'more lavishly, so that richer fare may be provided for the faithful.'** *(SC, 51)*

CONCLUSION

This very brief analysis of the major areas of the Lectionary leaves us with several key considerations.

Conviction

The revision of the Lectionary along the principles outlined was a major undertaking but by common consent it stands as one of the principal achievements of the entire liturgical reform. It is worth noting in passing that all of the major Protestant communities in North America have recently revised their lectionaries, and all of them have adopted the principles of the Roman one. Our first response to the Lectionary should be one of conviction: it is through the Lectionary that **'God speaks to his people of redemption and salvation and nourishes their spirit, Christ is present among the faithful through his word.'** *(SC 33)*

Preparation

In outlining the basic principles we have had some indication of the richness of the Lectionary, both in its actual content of the fundamental scriptural presentation, and in its potential for the expansion of that into a three year cycle which covers every aspect of the Church's teaching. The scale of work in getting all this across is gigantic, and demands preparation.

Familiarity with Scripture & overview

If the Lectionary is to fulfill its potential, it must be seen as more than the collection of liturgical readings: the ordering and structuring of those readings, whether according to season, or according to author must be grouped. Each part of the year, each season, has its own character, themes, ideas. It is important first to grasp these in their entirety, to have an overview. Everything else is merely a development of that. This means we have to become familiar with scripture. That may seem too tall an order, but it seems more reasonably attainable when we remember that the Lectionary operates over a three year cycle. All that is necessary is to become familiar with Matthew one year, Mark the next, and Luke the one after that. What follows is offered as a contribution towards achieving both that familiarity, and that overview.

THE CHURCH'S YEAR

Easter — the centre and climax

When we look at the Lectionary to see how it works its way through the Church's liturgical year, there are few surprises in the sequence of celebrations:

—Season of Advent
(first Sunday of Advent to December 24 morning);

—Season of Christmas
(December 24 evening to Sunday after Epiphany i.e. to Baptism of our Lord);

—Season of Lent
(Ash Wednesday to Saturday of 5th week of Lent);

—Holy Week
(Passion Sunday to Holy Thursday Chrism Mass);
—Easter Triduum and Eastertide
(Holy Thursday Mass of the Lord's Supper to Pentecost Sunday)
—Ordinary Time
(Monday after the Baptism of our Lord to Saturday of the last week);
—Solemnities of the Lord
(Trinity Sunday, Corpus Christi, Sacred Heart of Jesus);
—Proper of the Saints;
—Common Masses;
—Ritual Masses;
—Votive Masses

This layout seems to follow, more or less, the way we are accustomed to thinking of the cycle of liturgical celebration of the mystery of Christ as beginning on the first Sunday of Advent and running through to the last Sunday of the year.

In fact, the lectionary is based on a Calendar which was revised at the command of Vatican II: **'the liturgical year is to be revised so that the traditional customs and disciplines of sacred seasons can be preserved or restored to meet the conditions of modern times; their specific character is to be retained, so that they duly nourish the piety of the faithful who celebrate the mysteries of Christian redemption, *and above all the Paschal mystery . . .*'** *(SC 107).*

The consequences of that revision, though implicit throughout the Lectionary, are clearly and explicitly set out in the revised Calendar. Put briefly, the intention behind the revised calendar is to put into practice the theory or principle that we have always held and assented, namely, that ***Easter is the centre of the Church's year***. The papal document which promulgated the Calendar in 1969 is entitled *The Celebration of the Paschal Mystery*, and this is no mere coincidence; to a large extent, it sums up the general direction and controlling thought behind this particular reform: **'We are clearly instructed by the Second Vatican Council that the celebration of the Paschal Mystery is of the greatest importance in Christian liturgical worship, and that it unfolds throughout the course of days, weeks, and the whole year. From this it follows that the Paschal Mystery should receive greater prominence in the revision of the liturgical calendar.'** *(MPC).*

So it is that the Calendar itself sets out the year in an order of

importance, rather than the chronological order which we are used to:
the Paschal Triduum;
Easter Time;
Lent;
Christmas Time;
Advent;
Ordinary Time;
and finally, the Ember and Rogation days.
(CR 17-47)

The revised *Roman Calendar* was merely a skeleton; it was fleshed out by the liturgical books themselves, that is, by the Roman Missal of Paul VI, by the Lectionary, by the revised sacramental rites, and by the revised Divine Office. But of all these, it is the Lectionary, by providing the liturgy of the word for the particular celebration in whatever season, that sets the tone and mood of our celebration. Implicit in the readings the Lectionary provides, and which we must appreciate if we are to understand what the Lectionary is trying to achieve is this sense of perspective: ***the rest of the seasons and the rest of the year is set firmly in its relation to Easter, and is geared to the fullness of our celebration of Easter***: and Easter itself focuses on the Easter Triduum, particularly the Paschal Vigil which is **'most blessed of all nights . . . when Jesus Christ broke the chains of death and rose triumphant from the grave . . . our true passover feast . . .'** *(Easter Preconium)*

The key-stone in all of Vatican II's reform and revision is the basic idea that **'the liturgy is the *summit* towards which the activity of the Church is directed; at the same time, it is the *fountain* from which all her power flows.'** *(SC 10)*. Within that we have to see that the liturgy itself, through the Lectionary as much as anything else, makes Easter the 'summit and fountain' for the rest of the year.

To make this implicit principle as obvious as possible, this guide to the Lectionary follows in as practical a way as is possible, that order of importance:

PART 1 — THE SEASON OF JOHN
LENT-EASTER

1. **Introduction to the 'Season of John'**
2. **Lent**
3. **The Easter Triduum**
4. **Easter Time**

Part 1
The Season of John
Lent-Easter

Part 1
The Season of John
Lent-Easter

LENT

The theology of John's Gospel

The Gospel of John is rich and profound: it has been likened to a great symphony, with its development of themes, underlying points of reference to which it comes back time and time again, with its overture and its finale; it has been likened to a great work of art, with its multiple use of colours, textures, light and shade — all held together by the master plan in the mind of the artist. Perhaps it could be thought of as an archaeological 'dig', where we constantly uncover further strata, ever deeper levels of thought and expression.

One obvious level of thought is the ***'liturgical level'***; it is obvious because John goes out of his way to relate the life and ministry of Jesus to the ongoing liturgical life of Israel, and the significant events of Jesus' life are presented against the backdrop of the different feasts and their meaning. Passover, Dedication, Tabernacles — we find them all; they quickly fit into a fairly rigid pattern which begins with the feast, includes an encounter between Jesus and the men of his time, and develops into a debate, controversy, or discourse. This is perhaps most noticeable in John's timing and sequence in the passion and resurrection narratives: these events are presented in close relation to the celebration of the Passover. In terms of what we can understand of the message of the Fourth Gospel, it is clear that the more we know and appreciate about the liturgical life of Israel and the significance of the different feasts, the more we will understand and appreciate John's intention.

A further level of thought is the '***level of personal encounters***', which clearly hold an important place in the evangelist's view of the Gospel story. The first disciples, Nicodemus, the Samaritan Woman, the paralytic at the pool, the man born blind, and others — they all represent some aspect of the force and power of the confrontation between the Word and men. Above all, there is written into the Gospel the most important encounter of all: the evangelist himself has met Christ and his life has been changed, and his intention is that through his work his readers should experience something of the same force and power.

A third level of thought is perhaps one that causes most difficulty — what could be termed the '***level of symbolism***'. It demands a certain degree of perception to be aware that John never mentions anything for its own sake, but always for the symbolic value that it has. The six water-pots at Cana, from symbols of the Jewish rites of purification, become symbols of the abundance and quality of the new creation in Christ; the clay placed on the eyes of the man born blind by Christ becomes likewise a symbol of a new creation. Throughout the Gospel there are these symbolic references, and it may be that far from proving a further obstacle to our understanding, they are a positive aid; it may be that we can recognise that this evangelist shares with the artist, the dramatist, the novelist of our own times that special quality which has been called 'Poet's Eye'.

There is another level which is peculiar to John's Gospel, which could be called the '***level of synthesis***', where the evangelist tries to sum up in one sentence or phrase the total reality of the mystery of Christ. We can see this at work especially in the 'auto-definitions' of Jesus: the Bread of Life; the Light of the World; the Good Shepherd; the True Vine; the Sheepgate; the Way, the Truth, and the Life; the Resurrection and the Life — they are all so many attempts to get at the heart of what the evangelist is wanting to say. Each of them opens up for us that chance of a fuller understanding of Christ which makes for a fuller, adult, Christian life.

If asked to sum up what the Gospel of John is about, it seems that the answer would have to be that John's is the 'Gospel of Life'. The fullness of life, which is characteristic of the inner life of God himself, is now incarnate in Christ and through his humanity is communicated to men. This basic principle explains why the personal encounters feature so much in the liturgy of Lent, because each of them demonstrates some aspect of this fullness of life, and the total picture goes a long way to providing an understanding of what baptism is as the Sacrament of Life, the beginning of the life of grace. The connection between baptism and the resurrection is also worked out in John: every incident in the Gospel is charged with the power of the Risen Lord, and the 'life' which comes to men through the Risen Lord is already here and now the beginning of 'eternal life'. In the work of John, we can see a theology of grace which is not worked out in abstract ideas, but rather through the experience of individuals like ourselves.

The structure of John's Gospel

One point above all else is worth making when it comes to defining the fourth gospel — it is a 'gospel' every bit as much as the others are. Like the others, it is an account of the Good News of Jesus Christ in whom is salvation and life. It is an ordered and developed account of the faith of the Church in its Lord, based on the preaching of the apostles — its origins are to be found in the apostolic kerygma. This is already the key to its composition:

—the completion of salvation history in Jesus Christ, the Word of God incarnate
(Prologue, i.e. 1:1-18);

—the designation of Jesus as 'Messiah' through the descent of the Holy Spirit and the witness of John the Baptist
(1:19-34);

—the manifestation of the Word incarnate through his works or 'signs', and through his words
(the 'Book of Signs' i.e. 1:35-12:50);

—the narrative of the passion, death and resurrection, and appearances of the risen Lord
(the 'Book of the Passion' i.e. 13:1-20:31);

—an appendix which describes the commission of the Church to carry through the work of the Word incarnate in the Holy Spirit
(chapter 21).

These are the themes of the fourth gospel, and there is nothing there to separate it from the others. What is different is the manner in which these ideas are presented.

John's Gospel in the Lectionary

Precisely because of these theological features of John's Gospel, paschal mystery, the Gospel of John stands at the heart of the liturgy the end of the Easter season, the Fourth Gospel remains the major source for the liturgy of the Word; as the introduction to the Lectionary explains: **'the tradition of both east and west has been preserved by which the Gospel of John is read in the final weeks of Lent and throughout Easter time, because it is the 'spiritual' Gospel in which the mystery of Christ is sounded out to greater depths.** *(OLM 7)*

When we relate the various levels we were able to discern in John's Gospel to the way in which the Lectionary itself makes use of the Fourth gospel, then we begin to see how we might penetrate some of the riches which John affords us for an understanding of our own baptism and of the paschal mystery in its completeness.

First, we must establish how the liturgy itself is structured for this season of Lent-Eastertide.

LENTEN SEASON:

	YEAR A	YEAR B	YEAR C
LENT 1	Mt 4: 1-11	Mk 1: 12-15	Lk 4: 1-13
LENT 2	Mt 17: 1-9	Mk 9: 2-10	Lk 9: 28-36
LENT 3	**Jn 4: 5-42***	Jn 2: 13-25	Lk 13: 1-9
LENT 4	**Jn 9: 1-41***	Jn 3: 14-21	Lk 15: 1-3, 11-32
LENT 5	**Jn 11: 1-45***	Jn 12: 20-33	Jn 8: 1-11
PASSION SUNDAY	Mt 26: 14-27: 66	Mk 14: 1-15: 47	Lk 22: 14-23: 56

EASTER TRIDUUM:

HOLY THURSDAY	Jesus washes the disciples' feet		Jn 13: 1-15
GOOD FRIDAY	The Passion narrative		Jn 18: 1-19: 42
EASTER VIGIL	Mt 28: 1-10	Mk 16: 1-8	Lk 24: 1-12
EASTER SUNDAY	The empty tomb		Jn 20: 1-9

EASTER SEASON:

EASTER 2	Appearance to the disciples		Jn 20: 19-31
EASTER 3	Lk 24: 13-35	Lk 24: 35-48	Jn 21: 1-19
EASTER 4	Jn 10: 1-10	Jn 10: 11-18	Jn 10: 27-30
EASTER 5	Jn 14: 1-12	Jn 15: 1-8	Jn 13: 31-35
EASTER 6	Jn 14: 15-21	Jn 15: 9-17	Jn 14: 23-29
ASCENSION	Mt 28: 16-20	Mk 16: 15-20	Lk 24: 46-53
EASTER 7	Jn 17: 1-11	Jn 17: 11-19	Jn 17: 20-26
PENTECOST	The gift of the Holy Spirit		Jn 20: 19-23

*These passages are so important for the baptismal catechesis of Lent that:
—they are used in any year of the cycle when the rite of christian initiation of adults is celebrated;
—they may be used in any year of the cycle.

The emphasis in this presentation of the Fourth Gospel could be summed up roughly like this:
before Easter, it is the encounters which occupy the first place; Nicodemus, the Samaritan woman, the man born blind, Lazarus — each of them have something to tell us of our own life in Christ as a result of our baptism;
after Easter, it is the farewell discourses at the Last Supper which direct our understanding of the Paschal Mystery, culminating in the priestly prayer of Jesus and the communication of the ultimate gift, the Holy Spirit.

Implicit in all that has been said in this chapter is the essential and integral unity of the season of Lent-Eastertide. For simplicity of presentation in our closer analysis of the Lectionary texts, what follows has been divided into three sections:

— Lent (the five Sundays of Lent and Passion Sunday);
—the Easter Triduum (Holy Thursday, Good Friday, Easter Vigil);
—Eastertide (Easter Sunday to Pentecost Sunday inclusive, including the Ascension.

LENT

Introduction

Vatican II's Constitution on the Sacred Liturgy went out of its way to lay great stress on the need for a renewal of the Church's Lenten practice and catechesis:

'The two elements which are really characteristic of Lent — the recalling of baptism or the preparation for it and penance — should be given greater emphasis in the liturgy and in liturgical catechesis. It is by means of them that the Church prepares the faithful for the celebration of Easter, while they hear God's word more frequently and devote more time to prayer" (*SC 109*).

The text then goes on to explain in more detail how this is to be done: by restoring the baptismal features of the liturgy itself (which in many instances has meant a return to an older tradition) and by encouragement of practices of penance **'in ways suited to the present day, to different regions, and to individual circumstances'**. What has been said about Lent in the subsequent documents of the liturgical reform has really been meant to give practical expression to these general principles.

The spirit of the renewal was further spelt out by the commentary published along with the Roman Calendar in 1969:

'Lent should be returned to its noble simplicity and adapted to the understanding of the people, so that the less important aspects are seen in perspective, and the entire season regains its unique effectiveness'. (*CR*).

Among the various elements that go to make up this renewed Lenten liturgy, the readings have pride of place.

'The readings for the Sunday Masses were chosen to present to the people the prophets call to reptentance, and to provide them every three years with a synthesis of the total mystery of salvation; the gospel texts once read to the catechumens to prepare them for baptism have been reinforced. These readings are now directed to all the faithful, for during Lent the entire Church, together with those who will be baptised, recalls the mystery of Christian initiation'. (*CR*).

What used to be read as a series of texts for the benefit of catechumens has been re-introduced for the good of the whole community. So, there is a great deal in these readings about baptism: for those who hope to receive baptism, they emphasise the different grades of Christian initiation; for those who are already baptised, the point is equally clear — they must remember their own baptism and its responsibilities and they must do penance. The choice of biblical passages, therefore, has been guided by the 'thematic principle', in such a way that there is not only coherence between the various readings on any given Sunday, but also that there is a unity and coherence in the season as a whole.

There is an integral coherence which the Lectionary achieves not only between the Sundays of Lent in any one year of the cycle, but in the three year cycle as a whole.

This is achieved by centring Lent round the 'traditional texts'. To understand these traditional texts, they need to be seen in conjunction with the liturgy of Lent, that is, with the rites of christian initiation which are reaching their climax in their public celebration on the Sundays of Lent.

SUNDAY	GOSPEL	LITURGY OF CHRISTIAN INITIATION
LENT 1	Narrative of Jesus' temptation	Rite of Election, begins period of purification and enlightenment
LENT 2	Transfiguration of Jesus	
LENT 3	The Samaritan woman	First Scrutiny (during week following, Tradition of Creed)
LENT 4	The man born blind	Second Scrutiny
LENT 5	The raising of Lazarus	Third Scrutiny (during week following, Tradition of Lord's Prayer)

This is the traditional model of Lent, and it has been restored and preserved in the Lectionary. Remember, however, that the Lectionary operates over a three year cycle, whereas the traditional model was within a single fixed year. The Lectionary harmonises this seeming discrepancy as follows:

—for Lent 1 the gospel reading is *always* that of Jesus' temptation; and for Lent 2 the gospel reading is *always* that of the transfiguration. In this way the traditional model is preserved. But the Lectionary also manages to keep the quality of each year of the cycle intact by using the version of each of these episodes (temptation and transfiguration) which is proper to the year of the cycle: Matthew in Year A; Mark in Year B; Luke in Year C.

—thereafter, however the Gospel of John takes over as the dominant source: almost by instinct, the Church has turned to John for an insight into the profound meaning of the Paschal Mystery of the Lord's death and resurrection. So, the ancient tradition of the Church of both East and West has been restored in using the Fourth Gospel in the last weeks of Lent (and throughout the Easter season); the present Lectionary has cleared up a situation that had become a little confused, by ordering the sequence of passages in semi-continuous fashion.

More exact details of how John's Gospel is used in each year are given below, but there is one more general point of clarification to be made. The gospel readings for Lent 3, Lent 4 and Lent 5 in Year A are precisely those of the traditional model: the three great baptismal texts of the Samaritan woman, the man born blind, and the raising of Lazarus. Because of the integral connection between these three great baptismal texts and the restored rites of christian initiation which are celebrated on these Sundays, then these texts ought to be used in *any* year when there are candidates preparing for baptism at Easter. Further, to fulfill Vatican II's demand that Lent be clearly celebrated in a way that emphasises its baptismal character, the three great baptismal texts may be used in any year instead of the Year B/Year C readings.

The Sundays of Lent — Year A

GOSPEL READINGS

The traditional episodes of Lent 1 and Lent 2 are preserved, but the quality of the year is also maintained by using Matthew's accounts: the temptation narrative for Lent 1 is from Matthew 4: 1-11; the transfiguration account for Lent 2 is from Matthew 17: 1-9.

For Lent 3, Lent 4 and Lent 5 in this first year of the cycle, the Lectionary preserves the three great baptismal texts. They are each long gospels (the lectionary provides shortened versions, but only for use when there is a good pastoral reason), dramatically but simply presented, very rich in symbolic meaning.

OLD TESTAMENT READINGS

Throughout the cycle, the intention behind the choice of Old Testament readings is to get at the heart of 'the history of salvation', which is one of the major thrusts of the Church's catechesis during this season. In each year, there is a series of passages which underline the important stages of that 'history of salvation' from the very beginning up to the promise of the New Covenant.

In Year A, the sequence is

LENT 1	*Genesis 2: 7-9; 3: 1-7* The fall of our first parents
LENT 2	*Genesis 12: 1-4a* Abraham is called by God to become the father of God's people
LENT 3	*Exodus 17: 3-7* The people are given water from the rock
LENT 4	*1 Samuel 16: 1, 6-7, 10-13* David is anointed king of Israel
LENT 5	*Ezekiel 37: 12-14* The prophecy that God will raise his people from their graves; will give them a new spirit, and they will live

NEW TESTAMENT READINGS

During Lent the New Testament readings have been chosen on the thematic principle: they have been selected to harmonise with both the gospel readings and the Old Testament selections.

In Year A of the cycle, they all come from the letters of Saint Paul: three from his letter to the Romans; one from 2 Timothy; and one from the letter to the Ephesians. Because they are thematically chosen, they highlight one or other aspect of the entire celebrations of the word on any given Sunday: so, for example, on Lent 5, the promise made through the prophet Ezekiel in the Old Testament reading is seen fulfilled in the gospel account of Jesus raising Lazarus from the dead; but the New Testament reading pushes the application of the prophecy beyond the one individual (Lazarus), to Jesus himself, and thereafter to all God's people, because 'the Spirit that raised Jesus is within you'.

The Sundays of Lent — Year A

LENT 1

Gen 2: 7-9; 3: 1-7 *Rom 5: 12-19* *Mt 4: 1-11*

The Temptation of Jesus in the wilderness; through it all, he holds fast to the will of the Father. His obedience is contrasted with the disobedience of Adam and Eve. Paul draws the lesson for us: through the obedience of the Son of God, we find ourselves at one with God, restored to his friendship.

LENT 2

Gen 12: 1-4 *2 Tim 1: 8-10* *Mt 17: 1-9*

The Transfiguration of Jesus on the mountain; this all too brief glimpse of the glory of the Son of God will sustain us when we are confronted with the mystery of the Son of Man. Our faith, like that of Abraham our father in faith, will see the revelation of God's grace in the cross of Christ.

LENT 3

Ex 17: 3-7 *Rom 5: 1-2, 5-8* *Jn 4: 5-42*

The first great baptismal text, the Samaritan woman, brings us face to face with Jesus who will give us water welling up to eternal life. Like the water given through Moses, that given by Christ is life itself, the life of the Spirit, in which we can enter into the very life of God himself.

LENT 4

1 Sam 16: 1.6, 10-13 *Eph 5: 8-14* *Jn 9: 1-41*

The second great baptismal text, the man born blind, brings us face to face with Jesus, the Light of the World. The sight he gives us is true insight to recognise him as the one sent by the Father, his anointed. Hence our lives are to be suffused with his light alone.

LENT 5

Ez 37: 12-14 *Rom 8: 8-11* *Jn 11: 1-45*

The third great baptismal text, the raising of Lazarus, brings us face to face with Jesus, the Resurrection. In him, we are destined for life, the life of God himself. As we look to his resurrection, we are made sure by our faith that we shall also share in it ourselves, through the Holy Spirit which is given to us.

PASSION (PALM) SUNDAY
(Procession: *Mt 21: 1-11*)

Is 50: 4-7 *Phil 2: 6-11* *Mt 26: 14-27: 66*

The ministry of Jesus has run its course; it remains for him to complete the work he was given to do. As initial triumph gives way to suffering and death, we are made aware of the true significance of the Passion. It is, first of all, the fulfilment of the role of the Servant of the Lord, his chosen instrument of salvation. Secondly, it leads to Christ's glorification as the only Lord.

The Sundays of Lent — Year B

GOSPEL READINGS

The traditional episodes for Lent 1 and Lent 2 are preserved, but the quality of the year is also maintained by using Mark's accounts: the temptation narrative for Lent 1 is from Mark 1: 12-15; the transfiguration account for Lent 2 is from Mark 9: 2-10.

For Lent 3, Lent 4 and Lent 5 in this second year of the cycle, we revert to the Gospel of John. The passages chosen are where John speaks of the future glorification of Christ through the cross and resurrection. So, the sequence is this:

LENT 3 *John 12: 13-25*
the purification of the Temple and the announcement of the New Temple

LENT 4 *John 3: 14-21*
the interview with Nicodemus, with special reference to 'the lifting up' of the Son of Man

LENT 5 *John 12: 20-33*
the very important saying about the grain of wheat which must die if it is to yield a harvest

OLD TESTAMENT READINGS

Throughout the cycle, the intention behind the choice of OT readings in Lent is to get at the heart of the 'history of salvation', which is one of the major thrusts of the whole construction of the Church's catechesis during this season. In each year, there is a series of passages which underline the important stages of that 'history' from the very beginning up to the promise of the New Covenant.

In Year B, the sequence is

LENT 1	*Genesis 9: 8-18* The covenant between God and Noah after the flood
LENT 2	*Genesis 22: 1-2, 9-13, 15-18* The faith of Abraham, ready to sacrifice even his beloved son
LENT 3	*Exodus 20: 1-17* The Ten Commandments, the seal of the Covenant between God and Israel
LENT 4	*2 Chronicles 36: 14-16, 19-23* God remains faithful to his Covenant in spite of the infidelity of his people
LENT 5	*Jeremiah 31: 31-34* The promise of the coming of the New Covenant

NEW TESTAMENT READINGS

During Lent, the New Testament readings have been chosen on the thematic principle: they have been selected to harmonise with both the gospel readings and the Old Testament selections.

In this second year of the cycle they come from a variety of sources: 1 Peter; Romans; 1 Corinthians; Ephesians and Hebrews. Because they are thematically chosen, they highlight one or other aspect of the entire celebration of the Word on any given Sunday.

For instance, the reading from 1 Corinthians is placed between the Ten Commandments and the announcement of Jesus as the New Temple; there is a great paradox here, and Saint Paul resolves it in terms of God's wisdom contrasted with human wisdom. The great problem for the early Church was the cross; the readings for Lent 3 push us in the direction of recognising in the cross itself a part of the overall design of God in dealing first with the chosen people and then with the whole human family.

The Sundays of Lent — Year B

LENT 1

Gen 9: 8-15 *1 Pet 3: 18-22* *Mk 1: 12-15*

The temptation of Jesus in the wilderness. While Mark does not dwell on this episode, he links it very closely with the beginning of Jesus' preaching ministry. The will of his Father takes precedence over everything else in Jesus' life. Like Noah, we are saved by the waters, in this case of baptism, which identify us with Christ. So, the Father's will must be our guide in life.

LENT 2

Gen 22: 1-2, 9, 10-13, 15-18 *Rom 8: 31-34* *Mk 9: 2-10*

The Transfiguration of Jesus on the mountain. Already the shadow of the cross looms large; for our salvation God will spare not even his own Son. Also, he will ask of us sacrifice just as he asked it of Abraham. This is the mystery of the Son of Man in practice; we are to learn of it like the apostles — the hard way.

LENT 3

Exodus 20: 1-7 *1 Cor 1: 22-25* *Jn 2: 13-25*

Jesus, the New Temple of God. He replaces the Law given by God to Moses, which is not destroyed, but taken up into the true worship 'in the spirit and truth'. Christ asks for faith above all else, a faith which is deep and personal, because he is the 'power and wisdom of God'. Baptism is only the beginning of our response in faith.

LENT 4

2 Chron 36: 14-16, 19-23 *Eph 2: 4-10* *Jn 3: 14-21*

Jesus, the Source of Eternal Life. The 'lifting up' of the Son of Man on the cross is destined for the salvation of everyone. Just as God has saved his people in the past, he continues to do so through his Son. Our response of faith, therefore, demands that we live 'the good life as from the beginning he meant us to live it'.

LENT 5

Jer 31: 31-34 *Heb 5: 7-9* *Jn 12: 20-33*

Jesus the centre of unity for the whole family of God. Face to face with the 'hour' of his passion, Jesus does not shrink, but carries out the will of his Father — this is why he is glorified; his death is the means whereby God reaps for himself a universal harvest. In him, God has made a new covenant with the human race, and so he is the 'source of eternal life and salvation for all who obey him' in faith.

PASSION (PALM) SUNDAY
(Procession: *Mk 11: 1-10 or Jn 12: 12-16)*

Is 50: 4-7 *Phil 2: 6-11* *Mk 14: 1-15: 27*

The final phase of Our Lord's ministry begins: the triumphant entry into Jerusalem underlines the true nature of his messiahship, in humility and service. Just how far that humility and service must go is pointed out by the reference to the Servant of God — no matter what the cost, the will of God must be done. The passion according to Mark in all its detail and brutality confronts us with the ultimate stage in the mystery of the Son of Man. But in his death is his glory and the centre of our profession of faith.

The Sundays of Lent — Year C

GOSPEL READINGS

The traditional episodes for Lent 1 and Lent 2 are preserved, but the quality of the year is also maintained by using Luke's accounts: the temptation narrative for Lent 1 is from Luke 4: 1-13; the transfiguration account for Lent 2 is from Luke 9: 28-36.

On Lent 3, Lent 4 and Lent 5 of this year of Luke, the emphasis is on repentance. The sequence is this:

LENT 3 *Luke 13: 1-9*
The call to repentance and the parable of the barren fig tree.

LENT 4 *Luke 15: 1-3, 11-32*
The parable of the two sons

LENT 5 *John 8: 1-11*
The story of the woman taken in adultery

OLD TESTAMENT READINGS

Throughout the cycle, the intention behind the choice of OT readings in Lent is to get at the heart of the History of Salvation, which is one of the major thrusts of the whole construction of the Church's catechesis during this season. In each year, there is a series of passages which underline the important stages of that History from the very beginning up to the promise of the New Covenant.

In Year C the sequence is:

LENT 1 *Deuteronomy 26: 4-10*
The 'creed' of the Israelites, given by Moses

LENT 2 *Genesis 15: 5-12, 17-18*
God enters into covenant with Abraham

LENT 3 *Exodus 3: 1-8, 12-15*
The call of Moses; his commission to lead Israel to freedom

LENT 4 *Joshua 5: 19-22*
The Israelites first Passover in the promised land

LENT 5 *Isaiah 43: 16-21*
God promises a 'new deed' for his people

NEW TESTAMENT READINGS

During Lent, the New Testament readings have been chosen on the thematic principle: they have been selected to harmonise with both the gospel readings and the Old Testament selections.

In this third year of the cycle they all come from the letters of Saint Paul: two extracts from the letter to the Philippians; one from his letter to the Romans; and one from both the first and the second letter to the Corinthians. Because they are thematically chosen, they highlight one or other aspect of the entire celebration of the Word on any given Sunday.

For instance, the Lectionary juxtaposes the 'creed' of the chosen people from Deuteronomy against Luke's account of Jesus temptation. It is Saint Paul's words that harmonise these seemingly unrelated themes, when he says 'Believe . . . confess . . . and you will be saved': the baptismal character is thrown into relief, for we are presented with the two poles of the baptismal promises — turning away from sin and believing the gospel.

The Sundays of Lent — Year C

LENT 1

Dt 26: 4-10 *Rom 10: 8-13* *Lk 4: 1-13*

The temptation of Jesus, culminating on the 'pinnacle of the Temple'. The profession of faith of Israel and of the Christian.

LENT 2

Gen 15: 5-12, 17-18 *Phil 3: 17-4: 1* *Lk 9: 28-36*

The Transfiguration of Jesus: a glimpse of the glory of the Son of God. The promise of the same glory extended to those who follow the way of Christ.

LENT 3

Ex 3: 1-8, 13-15 *1 Cor 10: 1-6, 10-12* *Lk 13: 1-9*

The history of salvation in the Old Testament becomes a pattern for Christ's disciples. A call to repentance, to produce the fruits of the kingdom.

LENT 4

Jos 5: 9-12 *2 Cor 5: 17-21* *Lk 15: 1-3, 11-32*

Christ, the reconciliation of God and man. The parable of the merciful father: the essence of the Gospel of Luke . . . a message of peace and joy.

LENT 5

Is 43: 16-21 *Phil 3: 8-14* *Jn 8: 1-11*

The mercy and pardon of God through Christ, the beginning of a new life for his people: forgetting the past, and looking to the future with Christ as guide.

PASSION (PALM) SUNDAY
(Procession: *Lk 19: 28-40***)**

Is 50: 4-7 *Phil 2: 6-11* *Lk 22: 14-23: 56*

The Journey to Jerusalem ends: the initial triumph gives way to the Passion of Jesus. This is real end of the journey, for it is in Jerusalem that Redemption is to be accomplished.

The weekdays of Lent

The rest of the season of Lent, that is to say, the weekdays, works out, from day to day the baptismal and penitential characteristics which are the keynotes of the entire period.

Throughout these weekdays, the readings are placed in harmony with each other, so that the different themes can be fully expressed. In fact, most of the readings have been retained from the Roman missal of Pius V (i.e. the scheme of reading in force from just after the Council of Frent until 1969).

However, from the Monday of the fourth week onwards, the Gospel of John is read in a semi-continuous fashion, to reinforce the baptismal catechesis of the Sundays.

However, from the Monday of the fourth week onwards, the Gospel of John is read in a semi-continuous fashion, to reinforce the baptismal catechesis of the Sundays.

Once again, the importance of the three great baptismal texts (the Samaritan woman; the man born blind; the raising of Lazarus) has been recognised. These gospels may be used on any day in the third, fourth, or fifth week respectively. To facilitate their use, the Roman missal provides an accompanying mass formula *ad libitum.*

Thus, the entire season becomes one great period of preparation for Easter; throughout the forty days **'the liturgy prepares catechumens for the celebration of the paschal mystery by the several stages of Christian initiation; it also prepares the faithful, who recall their baptism and do penance in preparation for Easter'** *(CR 7).*

EASTER TRIDUUM

Introduction

In its presentation of the Church's year, the Roman Calendar begins with the Easter Triduum. The reason for this is clear:
'Christ redeemed mankind and gave perfect glory to God principally through his paschal mystery: by dying he destroyed our death, and by rising, he restored our life. The Easter Triduum of the passion and resurrection of Christ is thus the culmination of the entire liturgical year. *(CR 18)*

Likewise, the Calendar is at pains to set forth the extent of the Easter Triduum: it starts with the evening Mass of the Lord's Supper, reaches its climax in the Paschal Vigil, and closes with evening prayer on Easter Sunday. The readings which have been chosen for this intense period are intended to express its importance and its unity.

It is worth noting that the first three days of Holy Week no longer present the different versions of the passion in turn; instead, they concentrate attention on the events immediately prior to the passion. But, by taking the poems of the Suffering Servant as a point of reference, they underline the theology of the cross.

This Lectionary arrangement of the readings brings to its completion the work begun in 1951 and 1955 by Pope Pius XII; if there is one thread running through the whole process, it is the way the whole Paschal Vigil is thrown into relief:
'The Paschal Vigil, in the night when Christ rose from the dead, is considered the 'mother of all vigils'. During it, the Church keeps watch, awaiting the resurrection of Christ and celebrating it in the sacraments'. *(CR 21)*

And if the Paschal Vigil is the climax of the Triduum, or indeed, of the entire liturgical year, at its heart is the liturgy of the Word: literally a 'vigil of readings' where seven Old Testament readings are presented, designed to provide a brief catechesis on the 'history of salvation'.

The Easter Triduum

HOLY THURSDAY
EVENING MASS OF THE LORD' SUPPER

Ex 12: 1.8, 11-14 *1 Cor 11: 23-26* *Jn 13: 1-15*

The eucharist is the Christian Passover. The people of Israel celebrated (and to this day celebrate) their salvation in the sacrifice of the paschal lamb. The very first Passover, preceding the Exodus is evoked as a preparation for the liturgy's two New Testament readings. The salvation promised and celebrated in Israel's Passover is fulfilled in the sacrifice of Christ, but it is the salvation of the whole human race that we Christians celebrate.

Jesus' entire life and his ministry are expressed in his giving of himself in the eucharist: 'Take . . .' This in turn, is symbolised by Christ's gesture in washing his disciple's feet: this clearly underlines the esseaning of Christ's life and ministry — that he came 'to serve, not to be saved'.

The New Testament readings leaves us with the twofold command of Christ: to remember him by celebrating the eucharist, and to be like him in our love another.

GOOD FRIDAY
THE PASSION OF THE LORD

Is 52: 13-53: 12 *Heb 4: 14-16, 5: 7-9* *Jn 18: 1-19: 42*

Jesus completely fulfills the mission of the 'Servant of the Lord'; the Son of Man is 'lifted up'. In John's hands, the passion becomes a triumph; from the cross Jesus begins to exercise his kingly power, drawing all to himself; he is the High Priest, offering and offered to his Father, for the external salvation of all of us.

HOLY SATURDAY
THE PASCHAL VIGIL

Gen 1: 1-22 *Gen 22: 1-18* *Ex 14: 15-15: 1*
Is 54: 5-14 *Is 55: 1-11* *Bar 3: 9-15, 32-4: 4* *Ez 36: 16-28*
Rom 6: 3-11
Year A: Mt 28: 1-10 *Year B: Mk 16: 1-8* *Year C: Lk 24: 1-12*

This vast range of readership presents the whole sweep of the history of salvation; the salient moments have been picked out with care, to emphasise the continuity of God's action in history. From creation itself, to the sacrifice of Abraham; from the crucial events of Exodus, to the message of love and forgiveness preached by the prophets; from the renewal of the covenant in each successive age to the gift of the Spirit of God and the power of his Word.

So the Law and the prophets bear witness to the great hopes and aspirations of God's chosen people. The New Testament is equally eloquent in its identification of the work of Christ as the fulfilment of those hopes and aspirations. Running through the Old Testament is the basic message of God's desire and action for reconciliation and restoration. God and the human race are gradually brought together. Their movement reaches its climax and is achieved in the paschal mystery — the mystery that makes present and active the reality of salvation of Christ's death and resurrection. It is through baptism that the experience of reconciliation begins — it is our personal sharing in that saving paschal mystery. Baptism also marks the beginnings of the Church's life with its risen Lord.

Just as we can never hope to understand the life of a Christian without direct reference to the paschal mystery, so we will not understand the mystery itself without a direct contact with the way God himself prepared his people to receive it. We are asked to see the New Covenant between God and the human race in Christ: the key to that is seeing it as the purpose and fulfilment of the Old Covenant. That is why the Lectionary presents this clear conspectus of the 'history of salvation'.

Provision is made for an abbreviation of the vigil of readings: for good pastoral reasons the number of Old Testament readings may be reduced to three, of which one **must** be the crucial Exodus 14. But if we see what the Church is trying to do in presenting this vigil of readings, our efforts will be directed to presenting the vigil in its entirety.

To communicate this wealth of riches to the people of God constitutes a real challenge to the preacher and the reader. However, there is a valuable aid in that each of the three days also enshrines a liturgical action which will help in this communication: the washing of the feet on Holy Thursday, the veneration of the Cross on Good Friday, and the celebration of baptism on Holy Saturday. It may help, too, to perceive the overall plan of the Lectionary's treatment of the paschal mystery. A challenge it may be, but it has to be met if the Word of God is not to 'return empty without carrying out God's will and succeeding in what it was sent to do' *(Isaiah 55, 11)*.

EASTER
Introduction

The *Roman Calendar* defines the quality of the season of Easter in these words:

'The fifty days from Easter Sunday to Pentecost are celebrated as one feast day, sometimes called *"the Great Sunday"* . . .'

'The singing of the *alleluia* is a characteristic of these days. The Sundays of this season are counted as *the Sundays of Easter* . . .'

'The first eight days of the Easter season form the octave of Easter and are celebrated as solemnities of the Lord. The Ascension is celebrated on the fortieth day after Easter . . .'

'The weekdays after the Ascension to Saturday before Pentecost inclusive are a preparation for the coming of the Holy Spirit.' *(CR 22-29)*

What the Lectionary sets out to do during this time is to dwell at greater length and to spell out in greater detail the mysteries of the Easter Triduum. So, many of the readings are concerned with the practical consequences of the paschal mystery in the life and worship of the Church.

GOSPEL READINGS

The Lectionary preserves the sense of unity that there ought to be about the season of Easter, in order that we might celebrate it **'as one feast day'**. It does this by imposing a pattern on the Sunday gospel readings, which offer an opportunity to deepen our understanding of different aspects of the Paschal Mystery.

EASTER 2	The Sunday of Saint Thomas.
EASTER 3	The Sunday of the risen Lord's appearance.
EASTER 4	The Sunday of the Good Shepherd.
EASTER 5	The Sunday of ministry and service in the Church.
EASTER 6	The Sunday of mission in the Church.
EASTER 7	The Sunday of the priestly prayer of Jesus.

This construction emphasises the fact that the Church has always turned to John for an insight into the deeper meaning of the death and resurrection of Jesus. It also remains true to the spirit and content of the Gospel of John itself, because the whole point of the discourse at the Last Supper is to give an interpretation of the final 'sign', which is the 'lifting up' on the cross and the rising from the dead of the Son of Man.

This pattern, hower, does not enforce a strict and rigid unity: the material in the the readings is too much to permit that. Rather, it represents a synthesis, which is all the more valuable because of the many different facets and ideas it incorporates.

In all of this, we are able to see the Church growing in understanding and commitment to its mission. This is precisely what the liturgy is asking of the Church in our own time during this season: that we grow similarly, in the power of the Holy Spirit.

FIRST READINGS

The Gospel of John remains the major source of the Church's inspiration during this time; the insight it provides into the paschal mystery is the cornerstone of the liturgy of the Word. Side by side with it, however, the Acts of the Apostles is read — 'a custom the Church has always observed', as Saint Augustine remarked. The Acts of the Apostles is used precisely because it shows us the experience of the early Church, that is, of a community formulating their faith. We are invited by the Lectionary to model ourselves on that — to formulate a faith centred and built on the Paschal Mystery. These two, John and Acts together, should be at the centre of our preaching and instruction to give body and depth to this celebration of the high point of the Church's year in our communities.

SECOND READINGS

More than at any other time of the Church's year, there is a unity of purpose and expression in the celebration of the word. We have already noted how the Gospel of John and the Acts of the Apostles are used side by side: the middle reading complements them by being either further writing of John (his first letter on the Book of Revelation) or from the first letter of Peter (the focal character in the Acts of the Apostles' extracts). But the lectionary's purpose in presenting these selections goes deeper than a coincidence of protagonists: the spirit of joyful faith and firm hope which comes across from all these three sources make them specially appropriate for our celebration of the Easter season.

Easter Season — Year A

FIRST READINGS

The first readings from the Acts of the Apostles in this year of the cycle follow this sequence;

EASTER 1	Peter's announcement of the resurrection to the Gentiles
EASTER 2	A brief look at how the early community lived and prayed together
EASTER 3	Peter's preaching about Jesus as 'the Christ'
EASTER 4	The need to be baptised in the name of Christ
EASTER 5	The appointment of the first deacons
EASTER 6	Missionary work in the towns of Samaria
EASTER 7	The Apostles prepare for the coming of the Holy Spirit
PENTECOST SUNDAY	The birth of the Church

SECOND READINGS

In this first year of the cycle, all the second readings are taken from the first letter of Peter. The entire letter is a joyful exhortation to live holy lives and, even when persecuted, never to lose faith, but rather to rejoice at being called to suffer for being a Christian.

Easter Season — Year A

EASTER 1 (EASTER DAY)

Acts 10: 34, 37-43 — *Col 3: 1-4 or 1 Cor 5: 5-6, 8* — *Jn 20: 1-9 (or Lk 24: 13-35 at evening mass)*

'Seeing is believing'; the witness of the apostolic group to the resurrection of Jesus. This witness we are invited to rely on and to share ourselves. Then we begin the process by which newness of life becomes a reality for us just as it it did for the apostles. Forgiveness of sins through faith in Jesus Christ — this is the message of the Church for our age too, to be preached 'in sincerity and in truth'.

EASTER 2

Acts 2: 42-47 — *1 Pet 1: 3-9* — *Jn 20: 19-31*

The faith of Thomas confirmed by the sight of the risen Lord calls forth the blessing of our Lord on those who believe through the witness of the apostles. The Gospel of Life, to which the Church is bound in steadfastness and joy; and so the Church grows.

EASTER 3

Acts 2: 14, 22-28 — *1 Pet 1: 17-21* — *Lk 24: 13-35*

The recognition of the risen Lord in the 'breaking of bread' begins the process of reflection on the words of the Old Testament which have to be fulfilled. The preaching of Peter hints at the grand design of God which embraces each generation of the Church. Jesus is Lord; so we believe and so we hope.

EASTER 4

Acts 2: 14, 36-41 — *1 Pet 2: 20-25* — *Jn 10: 1-10*

The Good Shepherd. Jesus, the Gate of the Sheepfold, gives life 'to the full' to those who belong to him. In baptism, we begin to share in this life given by Christ, and come back to God as his beloved children. Our reaction to this preaching must be that of those who heard it first; and so the Church grows.

EASTER 5

Acts 6: 1-7 *1 Pet 2: 4-9* *Jn 14: 1-12*

Jesus, the Way, the Truth and the Life. Through him, we come to know the Father; through him, a place with the Father is made ready for us. Hence, the dignity of those who are built into God's household, a priestly people in the image of Christ himself. Through the Holy Spirit, the Church continues to grow.

EASTER 6

Acts 8: 5-8, 14-17 *1 Pet 3: 15-18* *Jn 14: 15-21*

The promise of the Paraclete. The Holy Spirit is to guide and strengthen the Church in the observance of the Lord's commands. The Holy Spirit activates the ministry of the Church, so that it can witness to the Lord who leads us to God. And so the Church grows, in mission and in service.

ASCENSION

Acts 1: 1-11 *Eph 1: 17-23* *Mt 28: 16-20*

The Lord with his Church. The conclusion to Matthew's Gospel provides another key to his thought; the Lord is alive and active in the Church. It has the task of making him known to the ends of the earth. Christ is the head and we are built into his body, the Church, for the salvation of the whole world.

EASTER 7

Acts 1: 12-14 *1 Pet 4: 13-16* *Jn 17: 1-11*

The High Priestly prayer of Jesus. His priestly task is completed; it is for the Church to continue his work, to give eternal life to the world. There will be trials and persecutions ahead, but the Church faces them with joy and peace of mind, in the strength of the Holy Spirit; and so the Church grows.

PENTECOST

Vigil: Morning Mass

Acts 28: 16-20, 30-31 *Jn 21: 20-25*

The end of the Acts of the Apostles and of the Gospel of John; the season has run its course, and the Church awaits the gift of the Holy Spirit anew.

Vigil: Evening Mass

Gen 11: 1-9 *Rom 8: 22-27* *Jn 7: 37-39*
or Ex 19: 3-8, 16-20
or Ez 37: 1-14
or Joel 3: 1-5

(At least, but any, one of the Old Testament readings is used.)

Whichever of these Old Testament passages is chosen, it will highlight the work for which the Spirit is sent:
to unite everyone in praising God (Babel);
to strengthen God's people in his covenant (Sinai covenant);
to give the life of God himself (God's people brought to life);
to call the family of God together (the promise of the Spirit);
(Notice how the symbols of these passages, i.e. tongues, fire, breath/wind, will be exploited by Luke on Pentecost.)

The role of the Holy Spirit in the life of the Christian: bringing us close to God and strengthening us in hope. Jesus is the one who gives the Spirit, now that he has been glorified. And so the Church lives with his life.

PENTECOST SUNDAY

Acts 2: 1-11 *1 Cor 12: 3-7, 12-13* *Jn 20: 19-23*

The Spirit, the Gift of Christ. The dramatic manifestation of the coming of the Spirit on the Church enables us to see what he does — the apostles become fearless witnesses. And so all of us, no matter who we are, have this gift for our own salvation and the salvation of others. And so the Church goes on.

FIRST READINGS

The first readings from the Acts of the Apostles in this second year of the cycle follows this sequence:

EASTER 1	Peter's announcement of the resurrection to the Gentiles
EASTER 2	A brief look at how the early community lived and prayed together
EASTER 3	Peter's announcement of the Good News to the people of Israel
EASTER 4	Peter's preaching in the presence of the authorities
EASTER 5	The beginnings of Saint Paul's life as a follower of Christ
EASTER 6	Peter's encounter with the mission to the Gentiles
EASTER 7	The choice of Matthias to be a member of the apostolic group

SECOND READINGS

In this second year of the cycle, all the second readings are taken from the first letter of John. The point behind this letter is to deepen our awareness of the motivating power behind the whole economy of salvation (whose climax, the paschal mystery, is being celebrated in a special way in this season): that motivating power is the love of God.

Easter Season — Year B

EASTER 1 (EASTER DAY) *Exactly as for Year A —* *see page 47.*

EASTER 2

Acts 4: 32-35 | *1 Jn 5: 1-6* | *Jn 20: 19-31*

The image of the primitive Christian community 'united heart and soul' is placed alongside the profession of faith of Thomas; just as that community shared a resurrection faith, so do we. This faith can overcome the 'world', because it is brought into being and fostered by the power of the Spirit of God himself.

EASTER 3

Acts 3: 13-15, 17-19 | *1 Jn 2:1-5* | *Lk 24: 35-48*

The understanding of the Old Testament in its fulfilment is an important stage in the discovery of the true meaning of Easter, for us as well as for the apostles. The People of God which is the Church is the inheritor of the promises made to Israel; this promise comes to its perfection in our lives of faith and service. It is an important theme in the stories of the risen Lord with his disciples, that he opened up the Scriptures to them.

EASTER 4

Acts 4: 8-12 | *1 Jn 3: 1-2* | *Jn 10: 11-18*

The Good Shepherd lays down his life and takes it up again. In this is the fulfilment of the mission that the Father gave Christ to complete and so in this he is glorified. Christ is, then, the unique source of salvation for everyone; hence, the early preaching of the apostles insists on this. For all those who believe in Christ, there is a destiny already mapped out — to be like God, to 'see him as he really is'.

EASTER 5

Acts 9: 26-31 | *1 Jn 3: 18-24* | *Jn 15: 1-8*

The True Vine. Our life is bound up with that of Christ. To be his followers it is necessary for us 'to bear fruit', not just by 'words or mere talk'. The true test is whether we obey his commands or not; the response of the newly converted Paul is a model for our own. In the strength of the same Spirit which is given to us, we are to witness to the life of Christ within us.

EASTER 6

Acts 10: 25-26, 34-5, 44-8 | *1 Jn 4: 7-10* | *Jn 15: 9-17*

The commandment of love. The love which God has shown us in Christ is above all else a practical love — it translates itself into action. Just as it broadens the scope of the Church, making it universal or 'catholic', it must enable us who profess to belong to that Church to reach out to everyone with the intensity of the love of Christ himself.

ASCENSION

Acts 1: 1-11 *Eph 1: 17-23* *Mk 16: 15-20*

**The second edition of the Lectionary (unpromulgated as we go to print) will almost certainly add the following alternative New Testament reading:*
Eph 4: 1-13

The mission of the Church. As the Lord takes leave of his own, the work of the Church begins in earnest; it must do on earth what Christ himself did when he was in the midst of the world of men and women. The Church is the body of Christ, 'the fullness of him who fills the whole creation'. As members of that body, we are to come to an understanding of the plan of God and to carry it through to its completion.

EASTER 7

Acts 1: 15-17, 20-26 *1 Jn 4: 11-16* *Jn 17: 11-19*

The mission of the Church. What has been received from God through Christ must be passed on through the life and work of the Church in all its members. Bound together in love, the Church is called upon to witness in every age to the God who reveals himself in Christ, so that God's love can be complete in us and in everyone who hears the Gospel.

PENTECOST VIGIL *Exactly as for Year A, see page 49.*

PENTECOST *Exactly as for Year A, see page 49.*

Easter Season — Year C

FIRST READINGS

The first readings from the Acts of the Apostles in this year of the cycle follow this sequence:

EASTER 1 Peter's announcement of the resurrection to the Gentiles

EASTER 2	A brief look at how the early community lived and prayed together
EASTER 3	Part of Peter's speech to the High Priest
EASTER 4	The beginning of the mission to the Gentiles
EASTER 5	The journeys of Paul and Barnabas
EASTER 6	Important decisions about the Gentiles and Paul's mission among them
EASTER 7	The death of Stephen
PENTECOST SUNDAY	The birth of the Church

SECOND READINGS

In this third year of the cycle, all the second readings are selected from the Book of Revelation, originally written to encourage Christians under persecution. The constant underlying emphasis is on the triumph of good over evil and the eventual vindication by God of his people. Because of its vision of that vindication as a heavenly liturgy round the lamb it is particularly appropriate for the earthly liturgy centred on the paschal lamb.

Easter Season — Year C

EASTER 1 (EASTER DAY) *Exactly as for Year A, page 47.*

EASTER 2

Acts 5: 12-16 *Rev 1: 9-13, 17-19* *Jn 20: 19-31*

The faith of Thomas confirmed by the sight of the risen Lord; the faith of the Church confirmed by the faith of the apostles. The Gospel of life.

EASTER 3

Acts 5: 27-32, 40-41 *Rev 5: 11-14* *Jn 21: 1-19*

Another appearance of the risen Christ. Peter's profession of love, a love that gives him and the others joy in suffering humiliation for the sake of Jesus' name.

EASTER 4

Acts 13: 14, 43-52 *Rev 7: 9, 14-17* *Jn 10: 27-30*

The Good Shepherd gives to his sheep the gift of eternal life. This life is already ours through the reception of the Good News which brings us joy and the Holy Spirit.

EASTER 5

Acts 14: 21-27 *Rev 21: 1-15* *Jn 13: 31-35*

The New Commandment of Love: we are to love with the love of Jesus himself. This is the love that overcomes all obstacles and gives us a newness of life in joy.

EASTER 6

Acts 15: 1-2, 22-29 *Rev 21: 10-14, 22-23* *Jn 14: 23-29*

The promise of the gift of the Holy Spirit who will teach us all that Jesus said. The Spirit guides the Church in searching for the freedom and peace of the Gospel.

ASCENSION

Acts 1: 1-11 *Eph 1: 17-23* *Lk 24: 46-53*

* *The second edition of the Lectionary (unpromulgated as we go to print) will almost certainly add the following alternative New Testament reading:*
Heb 9: 24-28, 10: 19-23

The Lord's return in glory to his Father manifested to his disciples. The commission to the Church to carry on his work on earth 'to all the nations', with joy.

EASTER 7

Acts 7: 55-60 *Rev 22: 12-14, 16-17, 20* *Jn 17: 20-26*

The High Priestly Prayer of Jesus for those who will come to believe in him through the witness of the apostles. Like Stephen, we too must be witnesses.

PENTECOST VIGIL *Exactly as Year A, page 49.*

PENTECOST SUNDAY *Exactly as Year A, page 49.*

Part 2
Advent-Christmas

Part 2
Advent-Christmas

Introduction

We have already seen that the Lectionary is essentially centred on Easter: Advent, then, like the rest of the liturgical year is set firmly in its relation to Easter, and is geared to the fullness of our celebration of Easter.

In the course of the liturgical year, the Church celebrates the whole mystery of Christ, from the incarnation and birth of the Saviour through to his glorious ascension, and on to the coming of the Holy Spirit and our expectation of the Lord's return. Consequently Advent and Christmas time assume a special importance as the first step along the way.

THE MEANING OF ADVENT

There is a double aspect to Advent that ought to be reflected in the way it is celebrated.

—it is the time of preparation for the solemnity of Christmas in which the first coming of the Son of God is recalled;

—but at the same time it directs our thoughts to the second coming of Christ.

That is why it ought to be above all a time of **'devoted and joyous expectation'** *(CR 39).*

Understanding this twofold meaning to Advent helps to offset the ambiguity that many of us have instinctively felt: Advent tended to be something between the penitential observance of Lent and the unrestrained joy of Christmas itself. At the very beginning of its development Saint Hilary is reputed to have called it *'the Christmas Lent'.*

ADVENT IN THE LECTIONARY

On the admission of the experts who worked on the revision of the liturgy of Advent, their work was not difficult: some elements had to be simplified: the choice of readings enlarged to suit the three year cycle; new prayers for many of the mass texts. As far as concerns the Lectionary many of the readings we already associated with Advent have been preserved.

But one thing the liturgical reform has done is to clarify the essential spirit and structure of the season:

'Although the liturgical texts of Advent give it a coherence and unity (which appears principally in the almost daily reading of Isaiah) it can nevertheless be distinguished into two clearly defined periods, both of which have their own special importance...

From the first Sunday to December 16th the liturgy expresses the eschatalogical aspect of Advent, directing our minds to the second coming of Christ.

But from December 17th to December 24th there are proper formulas for each day in the mass and in the office, that our minds may be more directly prepared for the birth of our Lord. The fourth Sunday appears from the readings at Mass almost as 'the Sunday of the Fathers of the Old Testament and of the Blessed Virgin in expectation of the Lord's birth.' *(CR 39)*

The two 'Advents' are closely related: through the memorial of Christ's first coming, our minds are guided to a consideration of his second coming. This double aspect of the season has governed the choice and inner quality of the biblical readings.

Throughout Advent the Lectionary will present an embarrassment of riches by way of ideas. Running through these there are two constant themes:

—the great deeds of God in the 'history of salvation' are recalled, and he is praised for them.
The Gospel and Old Testament will show us how God works.
—we have to see the effects of those great deeds in our own lives.
The New Testament will show us how we are to relate this to our lives.

Each of these themes has its own importance: the deeds of God are the basis of our Christian life; and that life itself is our response to God's action. Then we can speak with meaning of the 'coming' of Christ into our lives: the Lectionary offers the opportunity for us to meet Christ and be changed by him.

'In this Advent season, there arises the great problem of the encounter of men with God — *our* encounter with God. We know well what the solution to that problem is: it is Christmas, Christ himself, our faith, our Catholic life. That is why the Church proposes the Advent season to us through its calendar and liturgical cycle — so that we can understand the truth, not over and over again, but deeper and deeper. We are to grow up in our understanding of these fundamental ideas: 'When I was a child, I used to talk like a child, and think like a child, and argue like a child, but now I am a man, all childish ways are put behind me. *(1 Cor. 13:11)' (Paul VI, December 1971)*

GOSPEL READINGS

As far as possible, the quality of each year of the cycle is preserved. Only in the year of Mark do we find the Lectionary needs to supplement his teaching:
with an extract from John (Advent 3) to enlarge on the message of John the Baptist;
and an extract from Luke (Advent 4) since Mark has no corresponding section in his Gospel.

The overall structure of Advent, in every year, is the same, designed to run parallel in each year of the cycle:

ADVENT 1

The Gospels focus on the idea of the Judgement at the end of time.	*Mt 24: 27-44*	*Mk 13: 33-37*	*Lk 21: 25-8, 34-6*

ADVENT 2-3

The Gospels present the figure of John the Baptist, and his message: he calls us to repentance, to prepare for	*Mt 3: 1-12*	*Mk 1: 1-8*	*Lk 3: 1-6*
the Judgement of God which will be carried out by 'the One who is to come'.	*Mt 11: 2-11*	*Jn 1: 6-8, 19-28*	*Lk 3: 10-18*

ADVENT 4

The Gospels now focus our attention towards the birth of Christ by presenting the events immediately preceding it.	*Mk 1: 18-25*	*Lk 1: 26-38*	*Lk 1: 39-44*

OLD TESTAMENT READINGS

The Old Testament readings centre on the messianic hope of Israel taking shape and growing. The dominant voice is that of Isaiah: the Lectionary looks to him throughout Year A, and for all except Advent 4 in Year B. In Year C Isaiah is complemented by the messianic prophesies of Jeremiah, Baruch, Zephaniah and Micah.

As always, the particular prophetic extract has been selected to inform the Gospel.

NEW TESTAMENT READINGS

According to the thematic principle, these middle readings are harmonised with the Gospel and the Old Testament extract. This means they come from a wide range of sources — but they are all from New Testament letters.

For Advent 1 - 3 they emphasise the basic christian qualities that ought to characterise our waiting for Christ's second coming and God's Judgement: we ought to be living in hope and confidence, and in a spirit of conversion (metanoia), which should all be seen in lives of love, thanksgiving, joy and prayer. For Advent 4 the focus swings, with the Gospel, and the theme is Christological.

ADVENT

The Sundays of Advent — Year A

ADVENT 1

Is 2: 1-5 *Rom 13: 11-14* *Mt 24: 37-44*

Jesus points to the coming liberation and judgment; this is what the vision of Isaiah had looked towards — the gathering of all men in God's kingdom. To prepare, Saint Paul says, the Christian life must be our guide.

ADVENT 2

Is 11: 1-10 *Rom 15: 4-9* *Mt 3: 1-12*

The coming of the Lord prophesied by John the Baptist; this is a sign of the imminence of the kingdom — Isaiah had already seen it from far. Paul recognises it in the life of the Church: we are to be united in mind and voice with one another through Christ.

ADVENT 3

Is 35: 1-6, 10 *Jas 5: 7-10* *Mt 11: 2-11*

Jesus points to himself as the fulfilment of everything the Baptist had looked for, everything that Isaiah and the prophets had taught Israel to hope for. These prophets and their hope, says James, are to be our models as we wait for the coming of the Lord.

ADVENT 4

Is 7: 10-14 *Rom 1: 1-7* *Mt 1: 18-35*

Matthew takes us to the heart of the mystery of the Lord's birth; this child is to be Emmanuel, God-with-us in a way that not even Isaiah could have fully realised. This is the Good News that Paul preached and the Church believes; from it springs our grace and peace.

The Sundays of Advent — Year B

ADVENT 1

Is 63: 16-17 & 64: 1, 3-8	*1 Cor 1: 3-9*	*Mk 13: 33-37*

Jesus points to the coming judgment of God, and so the call goes out: 'Stay awake!' But, it is a judgment of liberation — Isaiah expressed the great need of humanity. Saint Paul puts this in terms of the Christian life: the power of the Spirit enables us to stand firm.

ADVENT 2

Is 40: 1-5, 9-11	*2 Pet 3: 8-14*	*Mk 1: 1-8*

The strange figure of John the Baptist is placed before us; yet he is the beginning of the 'Good News', the source of consolation for God's people, because his work prepares us for the work of Christ. The root of our consolation lies in the fact that God is faithful to his word and his promises.

ADVENT 3

Is 61: 1-2, 10-11	*1 Thess 5: 16-24*	*Jn 1: 6-8, 19-28*

The figure and mission of 'the One who is to come' becomes clearer as the Baptist gives witness to him. God's justice, his faithfulness to his own promises, is already at work; it will be as clear as day in Christ. For that reason, we of all people should know how to rejoice and be happy.

ADVENT 4

2 Sam 7: 1-5, 8-11, 16	*Rom 16: 25-27*	*Lk 1: 26-38*

Mary becomes, in a way that not even the prophets could have fully suspected, the 'House of God'. In faithfulness to his promises, God not only draws near to his people, he identifies himself with them. This Good News is given to us to be shared with everyone through our lives and example.

The Sundays of Advent — Year C

ADVENT 1

Jer 33: 14-16 *1 Thess 3: 12-4: 2* *Lk 21: 25-28, 36-38*

The Son of Man at the centre of the universe and of the history of humanity. The fulfilment of human destiny: judgment and liberation.

ADVENT 2

Bar 5: 1-9 *Phil 1: 4-6, 8-11* *Lk 3: 1-6*

With the emergence of the prophetic figure of the Baptist, a new age of pardon and reconciliation dawns, which looks forward to the Day of Christ.

ADVENT 3

Zeph 3: 14-18 *Phil 4: 4-7* *Lk 3: 10-18*

The preaching of the Baptist opens up a new sense of personal and social morality. The Daughter of Zion rejoices at the coming of the Lord God.

ADVENT 4

Mic 5: 1-4 *Heb 10: 5-10* *Lk 1: 39-44*

The expectations of the world, of the Chosen People, and of Mary herself. The birth is nigh of the Redeemer who will make a perfect sacrifice.

The weekdays of Advent

As with its other major seasons (Lent-Easter) the Advent weekdays serve to reinforce the ideas expressed in the Sunday readings.

Reflecting the twofold nature of Advent there is a corresponding double series of weekday readings:
a first series, from the beginning of Advent to December 16th;
a second series, from December 17th to December 24th.

In the *first series* the point of reference is the Book of Isaiah, which is read semi-continuously. The Gospel extracts are then chosen in relation to Isaiah, until the Gospels begin to speak of John the Baptist: thereafter other Old Testament extracts are used which are closer to the theme of the Gospel from Thursday of the second week onwards.

In the *second series,* the point of reference is the account of our Lord's conception and the preparation for his birth as found in the two infancy Gospels of Matthew chapters 1 & 2 and Luke chapters 1 & 2. The Old Testament readings are messianic prophecies chosen in relation to the Gospel passages.

The solemnity of the Immaculate Conception fits into the character of the season very well, since it looks to Mary's motherhood as the source of all her privileges. This helps to highlight an aspect of Advent which has been commented on from early times: Mary can be taken as our model for Advent since this is the time 'of the expectation of the Blessed Virgin'.

CHRISTMAS

Introduction

'The celebration of the liturgical year is designed to exert "a special kind of sacramental power and influence which strengthens christian life" . . . and so as we observe the "sacrament of the birth of Christ" and his appearance in the world, we should pray that "through him who is like us outwardly, we may be inwardly changed".' *(MPC: the quotes within are from the 1955 restoration of Holy Week; Leo the Great's 27th Christmas sermon; Roman Missal of Paul VI — feast of Baptism of our Lord, respectively.)*

'The feast of Christmas places the Son of God firmly within humanity and human history, the centre in which everything is gathered together, and to which every human being has access for his salvation.' *(Paul VI: Midnight Mass 1976.)*

'The feast of the Epiphany resolves all our questions about our sincere profession of the Christian religion. It is a feast which brings into play the apostolic and missionary spirit, which, as the Council teaches us, must be characteristic of every disciple of Christ'. *(Paul VI: Epiphany 1976.)*

Christmas in the Lectionary

The basic principle governing the celebration of this season is that **'the annual celebration of the birth and early manifestations of the Lord is second only to the celebration of the Easter mystery.** *(CR 32)*

The Lectionary helps to create a strong sense of unity and coherence to the Christmas season by repeating the same scripture passages in each year of the cycle — with the exception of the cycle variations in the Gospel readings for the Holy Family and the baptism of the Lord. This, together with the fact that the Old Testament and New Testament readings are governed by the thematic principle means there is a single-minded liturgical concentration on the mystery of the incarnation.

The Christmas season — Year A, B, C

CHRISTMAS
Vigil

Is 62: 1-5 *Acts 13: 16-17, 22-25* *Mt 1: 1-25*

The coming of Christ is set firmly into the framework of the history of Israel. Isaiah sees this history as the history of salvation reaching out to its completion. Paul interprets the coming of Jesus as part of that same history. Matthew's genealogy places Jesus firmly as the son of David and Abraham, and defines him as 'Emmanuel — God-with-us'. Jesus is presented as the fulfilment of the hopes and desires of the chosen people, and the beginning of the life and work of the Church. The mystery of Christ is the centre of our lives.

CHRISTMAS
Midnight

Is 9: 1-7 *Tit 2: 11-14* *Lk 2: 1-14*

Luke sets the coming of Christ firmly into the mainstream of world history: thereby making the event one of universal significance. Isaiah's vision looks to the birth of the Messiah as the inauguration of the messianic age — the One who is to come will bring with him peace and light. Paul identifies this with Christ and demands that the Church, Christ's followers come alive with his gifts.

CHRISTMAS
Dawn

Is 62: 11-12 *Tit 3: 4-7* *Lk 2: 15-20*

The Good News of the birth of the Saviour is given first to the poor; it is by treasuring the Good News in our hearts (following Mary's example) that we can be built into a holy people for God. Paul puts his fingers on the power and motivating force of the whole mystery: the 'kindness and love of God our Saviour', which enable us to look forward to eternal life itself. Our lives are our reaction to God's action in giving us his Son to be our Saviour.

CHRISTMAS
Daytime

Is 52: 7-10 *Heb 1: 1-6* *Jn 1: 1-8*

John's meditation on the mystery of the incarnation brings us to the heart of the meaning of Christmas; the author of Hebrews takes along the same path. The Son of God become man is God's final Word to us. The salvation of God is present and active in the world — 'Good News' indeed, true 'consolation'. We no longer simply belong to the same family — we are God's kingdom.

HOLY FAMILY

Ecclus 3: 2-6 *Col 3: 12-21* **A** *Mt 2: 13-15, 19-23*
B *Lk 2: 22-40*
C *Lk 2: 41-52*

* *The second edition of the Lectionary (unpromulgated as we go to print) will almost certainly add the following alternative Old and New Testament readings:*
Year B *Gen 15: 1-6; 21: 1-3* *Heb 11: 8, 11-12, 17-19*
Year C *1 Sam 1: 20-22, 24-28* *1 Jn 3: 1-2, 21-24*

Year A Matthew uses the flight into Egypt to identify the Christ child still further — all is in fulfilment of the 'history of salvation'. In the light of this, we are to see our own lives caught up in the saving work of God: he has become like us in all things — we are to become like him, as his family.

Year B Luke uses the episode of the presentation in the Temple to identify Jesus as the light of the nations; but he also emphasises that the Son of God's experience is ours — he shares our life to the full. So we are able to take his life and the lives of those close to him as a model for our own family life.

Year C Luke encourages us to see the incarnation as the mystery of the Son of God within the human family. We are encouraged by the faith of Mary who pondered these things in her heart.

MARY, MOTHER OF GOD

Nb 6: 22-27 *Gal 4: 4-7* *Lk 2: 16-21*

Again, Luke emphasises that Mary treasured everything in her heart; so she becomes the model for the Church, and for the individual

Christian. It is through Mary that we have been enabled to see the 'human face of God', our Saviour, and our Father. In his name we are blessed, to inherit his peace and his kingdom, to become true sons and daughters of our Father, in the Holy Spirit.

2nd SUNDAY AFTER CHRISTMAS

Ecclus 24: 1-2, 8-12 | *Eph 1: 3-6, 15-18* | *Jn 1: 1-18*

The theme of Christmas is again announced: the incarnation, the Word of God made flesh. This is the 'mystery' hidden from the ages in which God has now been revealed to us in Christ. Just as the Old Testament envisaged, he has 'pitched his tent in our midst', so that our lives may be changed. It is a mystery to give us hope, and our hope looks forward to sharing the glory of the Son which we have seen.

EPIPHANY

Is 60: 1-6 | *Eph 3: 2-3, 5-6* | *Mt 2: 1-12*

The mystery of the incarnation is revealed to all the peoples of the earth: a new centre for the worship of God is established, i.e. in Christ. The Good News is confided to the Church so that it may be brought to all mankind. Our faith is 'catholic' (universal), and our response cannot be anything less than all-embracing.

BAPTISM OF THE LORD

Is 42: 1-4, 6-7 | *Acts 10: 34-38* | **A** *Mt 3: 13-17*
B *Mk 1: 6-11*
C *Lk 3: 15-16, 21-22*

**The second edition of the Lectionary (unpromulgated as we go to print) with almost certainly add the following alternative Old and New Testament readings:*
Year B *Is55: 1-11* *1 Jn 5: 1-9*
Year C *Is40: 1-5, 9-11* *Tit 2: 11-14, 3: 4-7*

By joining the baptism scene with the Song of the Servant, the liturgy reminds us what kind of Messiah Jesus is: he identifies himself with sinful humanity, so that he may raise us up. But the cost will be his own life offered as a ransom. He is destined to become Lord of us all, but only by passing through death and resurrection.

The rest of the year, as the Gospel unfolds, will explain this to us.

While the feast of the Baptism of the Lord brings the Christmas season to a close, it must also be remembered that it marks the beginning of Ordinary Time.

This is important, because it means that at the very outset the purpose of the semi-continuous reading of the synoptic evangelist over Ordinary Time is made plain to us:

Matthew's intention is to portray Jesus as fulfilling the Old Covenant, in the New. He has begun by showing us the true nature of Jesus as Messiah;

Mark's intention is to bring us face to face with Jesus of Nazareth, Son of God and Son of Man;

Luke's intention is more universalist, he will present a catechism of discipleship.

There is a very real sense in which the rest of 'Ordinary Time' will be spent in working out the implications of what has been celebrated in Christmas and Epiphany.

The weekdays of the Christmas season

Like Advent, the Christmas season has a weekday cycle of its own which contributes to the complete expression of the Church's faith in the mystery of the incarnation.

The constant factor is the complete and continuous reading of the first letter of John. The Gospel passages are chosen not so much to relate to this first reading but to present as fully as possible the manifestations of the Lord. However, since the theme of the letter is the love of God, this serves to provide a thread running through the whole range of the church' s meditation on the mystery of the incarnation.

Part 3
Ordinary Time

Part 3
Ordinary Time

Introduction

By common consent, the period described by the Roman Calendar as 'Ordinary Time' is the most difficult. The major liturgical seasons (Advent-Christmas and Lent-Easter) all emphasise one or other aspect of the mystery of Christ; the subject-matter is clear, the time is limited, and very often too the biblical readings are familiar because they are traditional. This is not the case with the rest of the Church's year; each year we are presented with a sequence of thirty three or thirty four Sundays during which we are to try to communicate the Christian mystery in its fullness.

The fact that the period is designated as ordinary time ought not to lead us into thinking that it is somehow less important. The fact that it accounts for most of the year is already a clear caution. The fact that it presents a large part of the Scriptures in semi-continuous fashion is another indication of the central place it holds in the Lectionary's construction. The fact that the readings are semi-continuous means that there is a systematic and progressive quality about Ordinary Time which is not entirely obscured by the interruptions of it for the celebration of Lent and Easter and the replacing of certain Sundays by solemnities.

There are, in effect, two periods of Ordinary Time;
from the Sunday after Epiphany (Baptism of the Lord) to the Tuesday before Ash Wednesday;
and from the Monday after Pentecost until the Saturday before the First Sunday of Advent.

Gospel Readings

The important point about this construction is the fact that each year of the cycle is characterised by the semi-continuous reading of one of the Synoptic Gospels on the Sundays. So, the first year (Year A) is, in reality, 'the Year of Matthew'; the second (Year B) is 'the Year of Mark'; the third (Year C) is 'the Year of Luke'. During these weeks of Ordinary Time, these Gospels in turn become the centrepiece of the liturgy of the Word.

If the mystery of Christ in its fullness is to be presented to the people of God, then it must be with Matthew, Mark, and Luke as guides. The key to an adequate presentation of the mystery will be a clear perception of the ***structure and theology*** of each of the Gospels. This has the advantage of letting each evangelist speak for himself, of allowing his concerns and theological ideas express themselves, so that the individual Gospel portraits of Christ may come across with clarity. Since the cycle is unified it is the composite picture of cumulative effect which will be of supreme importance.

From that overall pattern, once it has been grasped, the salient ideas of the particular Gospel can be detached. These will become the substance of the faith that is communicated during Ordinary Time in that year.

The purpose of this is to provide us with a ***sense of context***, an awareness of the setting of each celebration within its liturgical framework.

Old Testament Readings

The old Testament readings are chosen in direct relation to the Gospel passages. They come from a large variety of sources, and their purpose is to highlight one or other aspect of the message of the Gospel passage. In many ways this can provide an answer to a difficulty that often crops up: the determining of the one central point of the Gospel. Some of the passages from the Gospels, for instance, represent catechetical units which are held together by a thread which is not immediately obvious in English. The Old Testament reading can help to underline the meaning of at least one of those units. It can focus our attention on one or two central ideas in the Gospel readings; this is better than the confusion and frustration of searching for a logical development from one to another.

An effort has been made to keep the Old Testament readings brief and, as far as possible, simple; but an overriding consideration has been the attempt to present the people with the more important texts. So, while there is no logical order in the way the Old Testament is presented in the course of the three year cycle, it would be true to say that its central ideas are expressed.

A statistical breakdown of the use of the Old Testament is given for each year of Ordinary Time in the relevant section. But it is worth noting here that in each year, the prophetic tradition is used far more than any other: an indication of the emphasis that the Church, through the Lectionary, places on Old Testament prophecy and what it has to say by way of an insight into the meaning of Christianity.

New Testament Readings

In Ordinary Time, the New Testament readings do not have any direct relation to either the Gospel or the Old Testament passages, but follow a semi-continuous pattern of their own. The exact arrangement for each year of the cycle is given in the relevant section.

In general, then, each year is an opportunity to present a different New Testament letter. However, because of its length and the range of different subjects it covers, the first letter to the Corinthians has been spread over the three-year cycle in such a way that it features every year on the first six to eight weeks. Similarly, the letter to the Hebrews is long and detailed, so it has been spread over two years of the cycle: Year B Sundays 27-33 and Year C Sundays 19-22.

Many people have found this arrangement to be a weakness in the Lectionary; in fact, it might be conceded that it is the biggest single weakness in the whole construction. On the other hand, before deciding to abandon the three reading principles too hastily it would be as well to consider the freedom the Lectionary offers the celebrating community in the choice of which texts to use. There are clear principles laid down, designed to meet the demands of genuine pastoral need and to preserve the overall consistency that the Lectionary is designed to foster.

Thematic Feasts

There are two small exceptions to the overall pattern of Ordinary Time. The first Sunday of Ordinary Time is celebrated as the Baptism of the Lord, and the last Sunday of Ordinary Time is celebrated as the solemnity of Christ the King. Because they both have clear focal points, the liturgy of the Word follows the thematic principle, so that all three readings are interconnected. Even so, the quality of each year is preserved as far as possible, as will be seen from the schematic plan of the use of Matthew (pp. 88-89), of Mark (pp. 96-97), and of Luke (pp. 106-107).

Part 3A
The Year of Matthew

Part 3A
The Year of Matthew

Introduction

Apart from the seasons of Easter, Lent, Christmas, and Advent, which have their own characteristics, there are thirty-three or thirty-four weeks in the course of the year which celebrate no particular aspect of the mystery of Christ. Instead, especially on the last Sundays, the mystery of Christ in all its fullness is celebrated. This period is known as Ordinary Time' *(CR 43).* Even though this period is interrupted for the celebration of Lent and Easter, it does constitute one single season; what holds it together in unity is the semi-continuous reading of one of the Synoptic Gospels. Clearly, it represents the bulk of the Church's liturgical catechesis through the year; *in this year of the cycle, the chief vehicle of that catechesis will be the Gospel according to Matthew.* The fact that the reading of the Gospel is to be semi-continuous enables the liturgy to provide a programme of instruction which is systematic and sustained. Because of the structure of the Lectionary during Ordinary Time, the Church's catechesis is, in effect, guided by Matthew's insight into the person and message of Christ. Clearly, then, an understanding of the main lines of Matthew's theology and of the structure of his Gospel is necessary if the communication of God's Word is to bear real fruit.

The theology of Matthew

Underlying the whole of Matthew's Gospel is the evangelist's conviction that the Lord is *with* his Church 'always — to the end of time' (28:20). It is this sense of the abiding presence of Christ, whom he defines as 'Emmanuel, which means God-with-us' (1:23), which has guided Matthew most of all in his work. Not only was the presence of the Risen Lord in and through the Church very clear to him; he was able to discern the Lord *at work* in the Church also. These two ideas explain why this Gospel was known for centuries as the 'ecclesial Gospel'. The nature of the Church, or better, what Vatican II called 'the mystery of the Church', and the sacramental presence and activity of Christ — these are the two poles of the theology of Matthew. They will become through the liturgy the poles of the Church's catechesis in the course of this year. In reality, Matthew is presenting us with an idea that has gained ground in recent years; first of all, his Gospel confronts us with 'Christ, the sacrament of the encounter with God'; secondly, he speaks of the life of the Church in such a way that we can recognise the contemporary idea of the sacraments as encounters with Christ. In short, it might be said that Matthew's Gospel leads us into the areas of ecclesiology and sacramental theology.

Like all of the Gospels, Matthew's is about *Jesus Christ.* He sets out to show how Jesus is, in fact, the *Messiah:* he embodies in himself the promises made to Israel, the realisation of its hopes and aspirations, the culmination of its history. It is in this area that the 'Jewishness' of Matthew's Gospel appears most clearly. But, the evangelist has combined the idea of messiahship with that of the *unique sonship* of Jesus — he is 'Son of God' in a way that makes him one with the Father. Intertwined with these ideas, and in a certain sense, holding them together is his description of Jesus as 'Son of Man', in fulfilment of the prophet Daniel's vision.

Hence, when Matthew speaks of the Church, he identifies it as the 'True Israel'. His logic progresses by three stages:

Israel rejects Jesus;

Jesus himself rejects the Israel of the Pharisees;

the Church represents the true embodiment of the ideal of God's People.

But, he goes even further than this: he speaks of the *shape* of the Church, identifies its *leadership* — the apostles, with Peter at their head. Just as the concept of 'authority' designates Jesus as the Son of

God, so it also designates the Church as the continuation of the presence and work of the Son in the world.

This is the root of the 'sacramentalism' of the Gospel of Matthew; because of his conviction that Jesus is the Lord of the Church, he speaks of the realities of the Lord's life and mission as they are present and real in the life of his community. Thus,

when he speaks of the calling of the disciples, he recognises the same gesture of Christ in *baptism*;

when he speaks of the mission of the Church, he sees it in terms of the Holy Spirit's action and guidance and enables us to recognise the same reality in what we call *confirmation*;

the authority of Jesus is essentially the power to free humanity from sin and bring it into a state of reconciliation with God the Father — an authority communicated to the Church, exercised in the ecclesial reality of *penance*;

in sending out his disciples, Jesus gave them power to heal in the same way that he did — Matthew recognises this as an integral part of the Church's mission, and we can discover the same healing presence of Christ in the *anointing of the sick*;

in drawing a portrait of the Church, Matthew makes it clear that the apostles (with Peter as their leader) are the source of all ministry in the community, and it is precisely this apostolic ministry that the Church expresses in *holy orders*;

the Church stands or falls by its union with its Lord, Jesus the Son of God, and Matthew emphasises that the union of man and woman in *marriage* represents the same kind of unbreakable unity;

finally, among all the different forms that the presence of Christ takes, there stands out the *eucharist* — the focal point which brings all the other sacramental gestures of the Risen Lord into perspective.

The beauty of this theology is that it is simple, evangelical, and capable of limitless development.

The structure of Matthew's Gospel

The structure of Matthew's Gospel is readily identifiable; like every good catechist, he has organised his material clearly. The chief characteristic of the first Gospel is the interest it shows in the *words* of Jesus; the Evangelist's portrait of Christ is that of the Master, the teacher of the New Law, the new Moses. This explains why from an early age, almost by instinct, the Church turned to Matthew for the teaching of the Lord.

What the evangelist has done is to gather that teaching and express it in the form of five major discourses or 'sermons'; it is these five units which constitute the skeleton of the whole construction. The five discourses are:
the Sermon on the Mount (chs. 5-7);
the Mission Sermon (ch. 10);
the Parable Sermon (ch. 13);
the Community Sermon (ch. 18);
the Final Sermon (chs. 23-25).
It is principally in these sections that we will discover Matthew's theology and insight into the mystery of Christ, for they stand at the heart of his work and everything else is built around them. It comes as no surprise, then, to find that these are the best represented parts of the Gospel of Matthew in the Lectionary for Year A.

The Gospel of Matthew in the Lectionary

In order to do justice to the intention of the Lectionary, the five great sermons will of necessity be the focal points of preaching and instruction. The narrative sections of Matthew's Gospel which are placed in between the sermons are composed in such a way that there is a unity and coherence in the whole work. Discourse and narrative stand side by side, so that the narrative chapters prepare the way for what comes in the following discourses. The recognition of the way in which the Lectionary has reflected the structure of the Gospel itself will enable preachers and readers to see what they are handling in context from one week to the next.

'From the Gospel of Matthew there stands out the shining figure of Christ the teacher of doctrine, the divine lawgiver, as he is shown in the mosaics of the apses of Byzantine basilicas. That figure dominates the Christianity of the early centuries and it was from Matthew's Gospel that they sought the words of the Lord Jesus which he spoke when he taught us humility and spiritual courage'. (Lucien Cerfaux.)

UNIT I	THE FIGURE OF JESUS THE MESSIAH	SUNDAYS 1-2
SUNDAY 1	The Baptism of Jesus	Mt. 3: 13-17
SUNDAY 2	The Witness of John the Baptist	Jn. 1: 29-34

UNIT II	CHRIST'S DESIGN FOR LIFE IN GOD'S KINGDOM	SUNDAYS 3-9
SUNDAY 3	*Narrative:*	
	The Call of the First Disciples	Mt. 4: 12-23
SUNDAY 4	*Discourse:*	
	The Sermon on the Mount (1)	Mt. 5: 1-12
SUNDAY 5	The Sermon on the Mount (2)	Mt. 5: 13-16
SUNDAY 6	The Sermon on the Mount (3)	Mt. 5: 17-37
SUNDAY 7	The Sermon on the Mount (4)	Mt. 5: 38-48
SUNDAY 8	The Sermon on the Mount (5)	Mt. 6: 24-34
SUNDAY 9	The Sermon on the Mount (6)	Mt. 7: 21-27

UNIT III	THE SPREAD OF GOD'S KINGDOM	SUNDAYS 10-13
SUNDAY 10	*Narrative:*	
	The Call of Levi	Mt. 9: 9-13
SUNDAY 11	*Discourse:*	
	The Mission Sermon (1)	Mt. 9: 36-10: 8
SUNDAY 12	The Mission Sermon (2)	Mt. 10: 26-33
SUNDAY 13	The Mission Sermon (3)	Mt. 10: 37-42

UNIT IV	THE MYSTERY OF GOD'S KINGDOM	SUNDAYS 14-17
SUNDAY 14	*Narrative:*	
	The Revelation to the Simple	Mt. 11: 25-30
SUNDAY 15	*Discourse:*	
	The Parable Sermon (1)	Mt. 13: 1-23
SUNDAY 16	The Parable Sermon (2)	Mt. 13: 24-43
SUNDAY 17	The Parable Sermon (3)	Mt. 13: 44-52

UNIT V	**GOD'S KINGDOM ON EARTH — THE CHURCH OF CHRIST**	**SUNDAYS 18-24**
SUNDAY 18	*Narrative:*	
	The Feeding of Five Thousand	Mt. 14: 13-21
SUNDAY 19	Jesus Walks on the Waters	Mt. 14: 22-23
SUNDAY 20	The Canaanite Woman	Mt. 15: 21-28
SUNDAY 21	Peter's Confession: The Primacy Conferred	Mt. 16: 13-20
SUNDAY 22	The Passion Prophesied: Discipleship	Mt. 16: 21-27
SUNDAY 23	*Discourse:*	
	The Community Sermon (1)	Mt. 18: 15-20
SUNDAY 24	The Community Sermon (2)	Mt. 18: 21-35

UNIT VI	**AUTHORITY AND INVITATION — THE MINISTRY ENDS**	**SUNDAYS 25-33**
SUNDAY 25	*Narrative:*	
	The Parable of the Labourers	Mt. 20: 1-16
SUNDAY 26	The Parable of the Two Sons	Mt. 21: 28-32
SUNDAY 27	The Parable of Wicked Vinedressers	Mt. 21: 33-43
SUNDAY 28	The Parable of the Marriage Feast	Mt. 22: 1-14
SUNDAY 29	Paying Tribute to Caesar	Mt. 22: 15-21
SUNDAY 30	The Greatest Commandment	Mt. 22: 34-40
SUNDAY 31	Hypocrisy and Ambition	Mt. 23: 1-12
SUNDAY 32	*Discourse:*	
	The Final Sermon (1)	Mt. 25: 1-13
SUNDAY 33	The Final Sermon (2)	Mt. 25: 14-30

UNIT VII	**GOD'S KINGDOM FULFILLED**	**SUNDAY 34**
SUNDAY 34	The Solemnity of Christ the King	Mt. 25: 31-46

The other readings

As is always the case with the Sundays of Ordinary Time, the Gospel is the point of reference; it should be, then, the starting-point in building up a clear picture of the message of the Liturgy of the Word for each celebration.

OLD TESTAMENT READINGS

In the Year of Matthew, the statistical breakdown of the Old Testament passages is:

4 passages from the Pentateuch;
3 passages from the historical books;
5 passages from the Wisdom tradition;
21 passages from the Prophetic tradition.

Notice the weight that the Lectionary gives to selections from the Prophets.

NEW TESTAMENT READINGS

In the Year of Matthew the semi-continuous pattern for the use of the New Testament letters is:

1 Corinthians	Sundays 2- 8
Romans	Sundays 9-24
Philippians	Sundays 25-28
1 Thessalonians	Sundays 29-33

Part 3B
The Year of Mark

Part 3B
The Year of Mark

The theology of Mark

Recent discussion has opened up again the question of the identity of the evangelist. The universal and constant tradition of the early Church was clear on the point: Mark the evangelist was the 'John Mark' known to us from the rest of the New Testament, who became the associate of Saint Peter, and who composed his Gospel after the death of the apostle (i.e. somewhere between 64 and 70 AD) probably for the benefit of the Roman Church in the first instance. Whether we can go from that to the identification of Peter himself as one of the original sources, and isolate a 'Petrine tradition' within the Gospel, is an open question. But, the early tradition explains one thing: the fact that in this Gospel there are a number of episodes which are described (by even the severest critics) as 'eye-witness accounts' or indeed 'narratives based on personal testimony'. The somewhat primitive nature of the text lends weight to the idea that this is the earliest of the four Gospels, a major source for Matthew and Luke when they came to write their accounts.

Mark's Gospel is short, and his way of telling a story is simple and very direct; but the simplicity is deceptive. As time passes, people are coming round more and more to the view that Mark was a theologian of considerable talent. He sets out to lead his readers directly to the person of Jesus Christ, and in so doing he is certainly not afraid to present them with the humanity of the Son of God in all its starkness. The whole story, according to him, revolves around the confession of Peter; this is the turning-point, the crisis. After Peter's confession of faith, the emphasis in the Gospel switches from the preaching of the 'Kingdom of God' and the progressive revelation of the messiahship of Jesus to the idea of the precise nature of that messiahship. For this reason, the second part of the story is much more concerned with personal attachment to Jesus and an understanding of the cross — the 'way of the Son of Man'.

So there is a point in Mark's Gospel where it becomes a catechism on true discipleship, and attempts to address the question of how the follower of Christ is supposed to react when faced with the world and its problems. The portrait which Mark presents is something like a diptych: on the one side the figure of the 'Son of God' and on the other the figure of the 'Son of Man'. Everything that he says is geared to this: that at the end of it all we ask ourselves the basic question 'Who is this?' and that we answer it for ourselves too. He does not dwell at any great length on the idea of incarnation, and yet he is at pains to show us God at work in the life and ministry of Jesus. The whole structure of what he has written is dictated by this interest, and he has done his work, like the other evangelists,

'selecting some things from the many which had been handed on by word of mouth or in writing, reducing some of them to a synthesis, and explicating some things in view of the situation of the churches'. *(DV 19).*

At this point we can identify the areas of Christian faith which the Gospel of Mark will lead us to consider:

Christology: the mystery of the human and divine in the Son of God.

Faith: how it comes into being, and how it develops.

The Church: a community of faith, living according to the Gospel.

The Christian life: how, in practical terms, the Gospel is to be lived.

There are other interests in the Gospel of Mark, but these will only emerge with familiarity as it unfolds in the course of the year. The Lectionary puts these ideas before us, and it is our task to relate them to the life and experience of our own community.

The structure of Mark's Gospel

From the earliest times there seems to have been a concensus to the effect that even though Mark was close to the sources, he wrote his Gospel without any clear plan or pattern. At the moment, there are as many different 'plans' of the Gospel as there are commentaries, and some have even despaired of being able to find a clear structure. However, recent work has made it apparent that at least the broad lines of his plan can be detected. Mark begins by introducing his main interest — the person of Jesus himself, and he then follows Jesus through his public ministry; in Galilee, on the road to Jerusalem, and finally in the Holy City itself immediately prior to the passion. The doctrinal or theological pattern is built on to this geographical framework, so that when the question 'Who do you say I am?' is posed, the crisis is reached. Peter's answer is followed by a prediction of the passion, and from that point onwards, the burden of Jesus' teaching is that the Son of Man must suffer and die; it is directed no longer to the crowds but to the disciples only.

There is, in consequence, a great emphasis in Mark's work on the death and resurrection of Jesus, so much so that it has been described as 'a passion story with an introduction'.

Perhaps the inner movement and structure of the Gospel can best be set out this way:

	I THE MYSTERY OF JESUS MESSIAHSHIP PROGRESSIVELY REVEALED	1: 14-8: 26
Stage 1	Jesus with the Jewish crowds	1:14-3: 6
Stage 2	Jesus with his disciples	3: 7-6: 6
Stage 3	Jesus manifests himself	6: 7-8: 26
	II THE MYSTERY OF THE SON OF MAN PROGRESSIVELY REVEALED	8: 27-16: 8
Stage 1	The 'Way' of the Son of Man	8: 27-10: 52
Stage 2	Final revelation in Jerusalem	11: 1-13: 37
Stage 3	The fulfilment of the mystery	14: 1-16: 8

This division has the advantage of clarity and respect for the text itself. When we consider how the Gospel of Mark has been presented in the lectionary sequence for Year B, it will be clear how this pattern has been respected. It can then be taken as a guide for a systematic catechesis from one week to the next during the period of Ordinary

Time. The detailed argument on which this structure is based can be found in many of the commentaries; perhaps its clearest form is that to be seen in the *Jerome Biblical Commentary* (42:4-5)

The Gospel of Mark in the Lectionary

The Lectionary spreads the Gospel of Mark over the Sundays of Ordinary Time in a way that faithfully follows the structure of the Gospel, as we have been able to discern it above. This is not for the sake of the structure, of course, but in order that we may be faithful to the original intention of Mark himself: the closer we can get to what he is trying to teach us, the more chance we will have of grasping the message the structure is designed to carry. An awareness of the structure will help readers and preachers to see what they are handling in context from one week to the next.

UNIT I	**THE FIGURE OF JESUS THE MESSIAH**	**SUNDAYS 1-2**
SUNDAY 1	The baptism of Jesus	Mk. 1: 6b-11
SUNDAY 2	The call of Andrew and his friend	Jn. 1: 35-42
UNIT II	**JESUS' MESSIAHSHIP PROGRESSIVELY REVEALED**	**SUNDAYS 3-23**
Stage 1	**Jesus with the Jewish crowds**	**Sundays 3-9**
SUNDAY 3	The call of the first apostles	Mk. 1: 14-20
SUNDAY 4	A day in Capernaum (1)	Mk 1: 21-28
SUNDAY 5	A day in Capernaum (2)	Mk. 1: 29-39
SUNDAY 6	The cure of a leper	Mk 1: 40-45
SUNDAY 7	The cure of a paralytic	Mk. 2:1-12
SUNDAY 8	The question of fasting	Mk. 2: 18-22
SUNDAY 9	Violation of the Sabbath	Mk. 2: 23-3: 6
Stage 2	**Jesus with his disciples**	**Sundays 10-14**
SUNDAY 10	Serious criticism of Jesus	Mk. 3: 20-35
SUNDAY 11	The parables of the kingdom	Mk. 4: 26-34
SUNDAY 12	The calming of the storm	Mk. 4: 35-41
SUNDAY 13	Jairus' daughter; the woman in the crowd	Mk. 5: 21-43
SUNDAY 14	Jesus rejected in Nazareth	Mk. 6: 1-6

Stage 3	**Jesus manifests himself**	**Sundays 15-23**
SUNDAY 15	The mission of the twelve	Mk. 6: 7-13
SUNDAY 16	Compassion for the crowds	Mk. 6: 30-34
SUNDAY 17	The feeding of five thousand	Jn. 6: 1-15
SUNDAY 18	The bread of life (1)	Jn. 6: 24-35
SUNDAY 19	The bread of life (2)	Jn. 6: 41-51
SUNDAY 20	The bread of life (3): The Eucharist	Jn. 6: 51-58
SUNDAY 21	Incredulity and faith	Jn. 6: 61-70
SUNDAY 22	Jewish customs	Mk. 7: 1-8, 14-15, 21
SUNDAY 23	The cure of a deaf mute	Mk. 7: 31-37

UNIT III	**THE SON OF MAN PROGRESSIVELY REVEALED**	**SUNDAYS 24-34**
Stage 1	**The 'Way' of the Son of Man**	**Sundays 24-30**
SUNDAY 24	Peter's confession of faith	Mk. 8: 27-35
SUNDAY 25	Passion and resurrection prophesied	Mk. 9: 29-36
SUNDAY 26	Instructions for disciples	Mk. 9: 37-42, 44, 46-47
SUNDAY 27	Marriage and divorce	Mk. 10: 2-16
SUNDAY 28	The problem of wealth	Mk. 10: 17-30
SUNDAY 29	The sons of Zebedee	Mk. 10: 35-46
SUNDAY 30	The cure of Bartimaeus	Mk. 10: 46-52
Stage 2	**Final revelation in Jerusalem**	**Sundays 31-33**
SUNDAY 31	The first commandment	Mk. 12: 28b-34
SUNDAY 32	The widow's mite	Mk. 12: 38-44
SUNDAY 33	The last things	Mk. 13: 24-32
Stage 3	**The fulfilment of the Mystery**	**Sunday 34**
SUNDAY 34	The Solemnity of Christ the King	Jn. 18: 33b-37

Use of John's Gospel in the Year of Mark

There is one peculiarity of the Lectionary's presentation of the Gospel of Mark which calls for comment: the number of times an insert from the Gospel of John is used.

JESUS' BAPTISM

The witness of John the Baptist (Sunday 2) is something that occurs in all three years of the cycle; a passage from the 'inaugural week' (Jn 1: 19-2: 11) is coupled with the narrative of the baptism of Jesus in order to provide a complete picture of the Messiah at the very outset of his ministry.

BREAD OF LIFE

The period covered by Sundays 17-21 (i.e. within the context of Jesus' manifestation of himself) is filled out by a major insert from Jn 6 to provide a fuller and deeper version of what is already there in Mark. In the vision of Mark's Gospel, the idea of 'bread' is of paramount importance in Jesus' revelation of himself. John's discourse on the 'Bread of Life' fits well into the context and spells out what is merely hinted at in Mark.

CHRIST THE KING

The episode of the interview between Jesus and Pontius Pilate from John's passion narrative is used on the last Sunday because it sets out clearly the idea of Christ the King in its spiritual dimension — something which is a conclusion from Mark, even though it is not explicitly stated.

The other readings

As is always the case with the Sundays of Ordinary Time, the Gospel is the point of reference; it should be, then, the starting-point in building up a clear picture of the message of the Liturgy of the Word for each celebration.

OLD TESTAMENT READINGS

In the Year of Mark, the statistical breakdown of the Old Testament passages is:

9 passages from the Pentateuch;
6 passages from the historical books;
6 passages from the Wisdom tradition;
12 passages from the Prophetic tradition.

The weight given to the Prophets reflects the importance such passages have in the insight and meaning they can give to the Gospel reading. Here are two examples of how this works in practice:

—Sunday 24 presents the climax of Mark's Gospel. But that Gospel presents no less than three ideas:
—Peter's confession;
—the first prediction of the passion;
—Jesus defines discipleship in terms of 'carrying the cross';
The Old Testament presents the third 'Song of the Lord': this harmonizes all three ideas by giving us a model for our own understanding of Jesus' messiahship.

—Sunday 26 presents us with a gospel that, again, has three ideas, but which are not at all clearly connected:
—the saying concerning the strange exorcist;
—a short saying on the reward of those who receive Christ's followers;
—the extended sayings on scandal.
This time, instead of harmonising all three ideas, the Old Testament passage guides us into concentrating on the first of those three ideas, where it speaks of the spirit being given to strangers.

NEW TESTAMENT READINGS

In the Year of Mark the semi-continuous pattern for the use of the New Testament letters is:

1 Corinthians	Sundays 2- 6
2 Corinthians	Sundays 7-14
Ephesians	Sundays 15-21
Letter of James	Sundays 22-26
Letter to the Hebrews	Sundays 27-33

Part 3C
The Year of Luke

Part 3C
The Year of Luke

Introduction

Outwith the major seasons and the solemnities, the Church's year is made up of a period of 33 or 34 weeks, during which **'the mystery of Christ in all its fullness is celebrated'** *(RC 43).* Since during these weeks the Gospel of Luke is to be read semi-continuously, they represent a sizeable contribution to the Church's work of teaching and catechesis. The systematic nature of the Lectionary's coverage of the Gospel enables the liturgy to provide a *sustained* programme of catechesis. From the middle of January through to the end of November, this instruction has to be guided by Luke's insight into the person and mission of Christ; clearly, then, an understanding of the main lines of his theology and of the structure of his Gospel is necessary if the communication of God's word is to bear fruit.

The theology of Luke

The Gospel of Luke could well be resumed in this one sentence: Jesus Christ is the Saviour of men. But, Luke himself would have been careful to add 'of *all* men'. There is about his Gospel a universalism, a vision of a Gospel destined for everyone, no matter how apparently unequipped, no matter how poor, no matter how underprivileged in human terms. This is what earned for Luke the title 'the Scribe of the Gentleness of Christ' given him by Dante. And so we find in this Gospel a great deal of insight into Christ which has a social application: the poor, the outcast, the rich, the business man, the housewife, the judge . . . all of them will find in Luke's Gospel the indications they need to reduce the Gospel of Christ to their own situation.

But, as in everything he wrote, there is a balance to be held in Luke's Gospel. His portrait of Christ is in the nature of a diptych. Balanced against the image of the compassionate and appealing Christ, there is the image of one whose demands are total, whose time is short, whose message is urgent. This explains why Luke's is also the Gospel of renunciation and of perseverance. In the long run, what he offers us is a catechism of Christian discipleship — with all its privileges and consolations, but also with all its dangers and temptations. Both aspects belong to the picture — they do not cancel out one another, but are complementary.

The structure of Luke's Gospel

When we look at the shape of Luke's Gospel, we can gain some idea of how he sees Christ and his mission. He sets out to tell us 'an ordered account', after 'carefully going over the whole story from the beginning' (1:3). The idea that holds everything together for him is the idea of ***movement*** and ***direction.*** His central point of reference is Jerusalem: there his Gospel begins and ends; his version of the Good News represents a journey from Galilee to Jerusalem, and this is completed in the Acts of the Apostles by the journey of the Church from Jerusalem 'throughout Judaea and Samaria, and indeed to the ends of the earth' (Acts 1:8).

After the Infancy Gospel (chapters 1-2) which plays such an important role in the Advent and Christmas liturgy, he tells the story of the Galilean Ministry (chapters 3-9) in a way which is roughly the same as Matthew's and Mark's. But even there we become aware of his own personal interests, especially in episodes like the widow of Nain and the sinful woman that he alone tells us about.

At the end of the Galilean Ministry, however, he shows his hand clearly: from that point onwards, Jesus is on the move. The whole of the central section (chapters 9-19) is cast in the mould of a 'travel narrative', describing the journey of Jesus to Jerusalem, to death and resurrection, and his return to the Father. This is all the more significant, because Luke has gathered here all the material concerning the Lord that he himself contributes; the central section of Luke is unlike any of the other Gospels. This, then, is where we find the essence of his theology. The rest of the Gospel (chapters 20-24) rejoins the common tradition, even though Luke continues to tell the story in his own way.

The Gospel of Luke in the Lectionary

Significantly, 19 of the 33 passages from Luke which feature in the Lectionary Sunday cycle for Year C are taken from the 'Travel Narrative'. Luke's vision of the journey is not a geographical or chronological affair — he does not go into details of times and places. What interests him is that the journey of Christ should be seen as an itinerary for the Church and for the individual Christian. 'The journey to Jerusalem is the way to glorification and suffering. But Jesus is not alone. His disciples accompany him on the journey and are bound through him into a community . . . The way Jesus walks is unique, but his disciples may follow after him along it' (Flender). What the liturgy is demanding of us, and what the Lectionary is helping us to do, is to make the same journey with Christ in the course of this year.

UNIT I	THE FIGURE OF JESUS THE MESSIAH	SUNDAYS 1-2
SUNDAY 1	The baptism of Jesus	Lk. 3: 15-16, 21-22
SUNDAY 2	The marriage feast at Cana	Jn. 2: 1-12

UNIT II	LUKE'S PROGRAMME FOR JESUS' MINISTRY	SUNDAYS 3-4
SUNDAY 3	Prologue. The visit to Nazareth (1)	Lk. 1: 1-4; 4: 14-21
SUNDAY 4	The visit to Nazareth (2)	Lk. 4: 21-30

UNIT III	THE GALILEAN MINISTRY	SUNDAYS 5-12
SUNDAY 5	*The call of the first Apostles	Lk. 5: 1-11
SUNDAY 6	The sermon on the plain (1)	Lk. 6: 17, 20-26
SUNDAY 7	The sermon on the plain (2)	Lk. 6: 27-38
SUNDAY 8	The sermon on the plain (3)	Lk. 6: 39-45
SUNDAY 9	The cure of the centurion's servant	Lk. 7: 1-10
SUNDAY 10	*The widow of Nain	Lk. 7: 11-17
SUNDAY 11	*Jesus' feet anointed: the sinful woman	Lk. 7: 36-8: 3
SUNDAY 12	Peter's confession of faith	Lk. 9: 18-24

UNIT IV	'TRAVEL NARRATIVE' PART 1: THE QUALITIES JESUS DEMANDS OF THOSE WHO FOLLOW HIM	SUNDAYS 13-23
SUNDAY 13	*The Journey to Jerusalem begins	Lk. 9: 51-62
SUNDAY 14	*The mission of the seventy-two	Lk. 10: 1-12, 17-20
SUNDAY 15	*The Good Samaritan	Lk. 10: 25-37
SUNDAY 16	*Martha and Mary	Lk. 10: 38-42
SUNDAY 17	*The importunate friend	Lk. 11: 1-13
SUNDAY 18	*The parable of the rich fool	Lk. 12: 13-21
SUNDAY 19	The need for vigilance	Lk. 12: 32-48
SUNDAY 20	'Not peace but division'	Lk. 12: 49-53
SUNDAY 21	Few will be saved	Lk. 13: 22-30
SUNDAY 22	True humility	Lk. 14: 1, 7-14
SUNDAY 23	The cost of discipleship	Lk. 14: 25-33

UNIT V	**THE 'GOSPEL WITHIN THE GOSPEL': THE MESSAGE OF PARDON & RECONCILIATION; THE PARABLES OF GOD'S MERCY**	**SUNDAY 24**
SUNDAY 24	*The lost coin; the lost sheep; and the two sons	Lk. 15: 1-32
UNIT VI	**'TRAVEL NARRATIVE' PART 2: THE OBSTACLES FACING THOSE WHO FOLLOW JESUS**	**SUNDAYS 25-31**
SUNDAY 25	*The unjust steward	Lk. 16: 1-13
SUNDAY 26	*The rich man and Lazarus	Lk. 16: 19-31
SUNDAY 27	*A lesson on faith and dedication	Lk. 17: 5-10
SUNDAY 28	*The ten lepers	Lk 17: 11-19
SUNDAY 29	*The unjust judge	Lk. 18: 1-8
SUNDAY 30	*The Pharisee and the tax collector	Lk. 18: 9-14
SUNDAY 31	*Zacchaeus	Lk. 19: 1-10
UNIT VII	**THE MINISTRY IN JERUSALEM**	**SUNDAYS 32-33**
SUNDAY 32	The resurrection debated	Lk. 20: 27-38
SUNDAY 33	The signs announcing the end	Lk. 21: 5-19
UNIT VIII	**CHRIST THE KING: RECONCILIATION**	**SUNDAY 34**
SUNDAY 34	*The repentant thief	Lk. 23: 35-43

* ***NOTE: Passages marked with an asterisk are found only in the Gospel of Luke.***

The other readings

As is always the case with the Sundays of Ordinary Time, the Gospel is the point of reference; it should be, then, the starting-point in building up a clear picture of the message of the Liturgy of the Word for each celebration.

OLD TESTAMENT READING

In the Year of Luke, the statistical breakdown of the Old Testament passages is:

5 passages from the Pentateuch;
7 passages from the historical books;
7 passages from the Wisdom tradition;
13 passages from the Prophetic tradition.

Notice, again, the emphasis placed on the Prophets as a means of insight and better understanding of the gospel message.

NEW TESTAMENT READINGS

In the Year of Luke the semi-continuous pattern for the use of the New Testament letters is:

1 Corinthians	Sundays 2- 8
Galatians	Sundays 9-14
Colossians	Sundays 15-18
Hebrews	Sundays 19-22
Philemon	Sunday 23
1 Timothy	Sundays 24-26
2 Timothy	Sundays 27-30
2 Thessalonians	Sundays 31-33